TRADITIONAL AND NON-TRADITIONAL FOODS

by

R. FERRANDO

**Director of the Laboratoire de nutrition et d'alimentation
Ecole nationale vétérinaire d'Alfort
94704 Maisons-Alfort (France)**

Foreword by Professor H. Gounelle de Pontanel

FOOD AND AGRICULTURE ORGANIZATION OF THE UNITED NATIONS

ROME 1981

P-86

ISBN 92-5-100167-7

Printed in Italy

TRADITIONAL AND NON-TRADITIONAL FOODS

Cover by A. Romano

FOREWORD

It is not easy to write a book on food that both summarizes the known facts and sheds some light on prospects for the immediate and long-term future. Prof. Ferrando has, however, acquitted himself of this task with grace and distinction. True, he has been closely concerned with this fundamental problem for many years.

As Director of the National Veterinary School at Alfort, his deep knowledge of animal feeding paved the way to his subsequent appointment to such highly responsible posts as President of the French Commission on Animal Feeding and, more recently, of a corresponding Commission within the EEC at Brussels.

Zootechnicians have broken new ground in the science of nutrition, and human nutritionists have often benefited greatly from their work. Moreover, in considering non-traditional foods, experimental trials on animals are certainly an essential prerequisite. Prof. Ferrando's encyclopaedic knowledge of nutritional matters, ranging, as it does, from plants to man, is what makes the present work so sound. But it should also be stressed that it is his capacity to summarize the facts and present his arguments clearly that should make this book readily accessible to everyone.

One should also be grateful to the Food and Agriculture Organization of the United Nations for understanding the need to make available, not only to nutritionists but to everyone concerned with food problems, particularly to those at government level, a work that brings together both current thinking and practical applications.

It is difficult to see how mankind in the year 2000 will be able to survive without having recourse to what could be called non-traditional foods. In a few decades, and perhaps earlier, these foods will no longer be considered non-traditional but will have become commonplace. Man's intelligence will finally triumph in the battle against world hunger. We should be optimistic in searching for solutions that will ensure that everyone has enough to eat every day. The myth that there is a single, appropriate natural food should be disposed of. We have to be creative and do away with food taboos. But, of course, one cannot expect to achieve this in a day, so to speak, since it implies modifying attitudes that have been passed down through the ages.

Numerous surveys carried out in various countries have consistently shown that the doctor is still one of the counsellors most people listen to. Information should therefore be directed primarily at those in the medical and related professions, such as doctors, nurses and social workers. Prof. Ferrando's book, if given wide circulation, should make a significant contribution toward achieving this.

PROF. H. GOUNELLE DE PONTANEL

of the Académie nationale de médecine
Former Vice-President of the International
Union of Nutritional Sciences

CONTENTS

INTRODUCTION

Food and eating are probably the two subjects that, in everyday life, give rise to the greatest number of myths — to "that which exists only by and because of words" [1].

Along with myths there are also taboos, errors, knowledge or distortions of the realities. It is true that, in matters of eating and food, the consumer cannot be fully competent since the information he has at his disposal is incomplete, tendentious and badly organized.

In the developed countries, the consumer is becoming more and more concerned about what he is eating, and the result is the "food fad boom" noted by Johnson (1973-74). This concern seems to be greater when the consumer is satiated and barely knows the meaning of hunger pains. In the developing countries, the consequences of certain (frequently justified) taboos, traditions or customs are perhaps less serious, though they often make help and cooperation that much more problematic.

One should, however, not generalize too much on this subject. The rise in the standard of living in industrialized countries sometimes leads to cut-backs in what is spent on food to the advantage of leisure activities, particularly those connected with the automobile. Even though developed societies no longer know hunger, as such, there are individuals who are, unknowingly, the victims of food imbalances that they provoke by linking the needs of the family budget to ideas on food and eating distorted by a partial or total lack of knowledge on nutritional matters.

This is yet another reason to raise awareness of nutrition, not only among the public, but also among politicians. Neither of these groups is fully aware, as yet, of certain realities, nor of changes in agriculture that have been necessitated by the combined effects of population growth and a rising standard of living. Primitive man, according to Leopold and Ardrey (1972), only had a limited amount of food at his disposal because of the toxicity of so many plants. The discovery of fire and the possibility of cooking food doubtless helped the evolution of eating habits and, indirectly, of man

---

[1] "Ce qui n'existe et ne subsiste qu'ayant la parole pour cause" — Paul Valéry.

himself. Man did not fall victim to the appearance of flowering plants dinosaurs were poisoned by since, unlike the mammals and insects, they were not capable of recognizing, and eliminating from their diet, plants that were rich in toxic substances.

Nowadays we are no longer worried by this problem, but the damage wrought by pollution, especially that of industrial origin, could once again place man in similar circumstances. Moreover, we simply do not know enough about the factors that influence human eating habits, which are often distorted by poor information regarding food. Animals accept, and even look for, uniformity in their diet. Even pet animals prefer this mono-tonousness, although it is sometimes upset by their masters who believe, wrongly, that it must be boring. Uniformity is fine when it provides a balanced diet that meets the specific physiological requirements. But it cannot be applied to humans for whom a varied diet provides a certain measure of security that basic requirements will be met and for whom uniformity means boredom. Nevertheless, this variety can still be relatively limited when it is restricted to certain foods for social or psychological reasons or because of some preconceived notion. An excessive daily intake of foods such as avocados or bananas, or diets too rich in meat, offal or fats are just as harmful as diets with excessive amounts of cereals, potatoes or cassava. Over a period of time, an unbalanced diet can bring about changes in the metabolism — and even provoke actual food poisoning.

Underprivileged social groups, unfortunately, frequently take to alcohol as an escape from difficult situations, a life devoid of interest and the absence of any hope in the future. This leads to dietary imbalances. Alcohol alters the judgement, and then the behaviour of the drinker regarding food and eating; in the same way, the availability of leisure time and the possi-bility of escape from the city can make a person's attitude evolve. In the latter case, the desire to escape the city is usually accompanied by a search for natural things.

But what is a natural food?

It is very difficult to answer this question. The people who propagandize or seek out such foods would themselves be hard put to answer it. Every-thing that corresponds to the usual order of nature or reflects nature or that has been constrained by nature is not necessarily good.

Poisonous plants and mushrooms are natural. The quail that eat the fruit of poison hemlock without harm to themselves are natural, but they are also dangerous to the person who then eats them with a delight that is, sadly, of short duration. Natural food will reflect the imperfections of the soil where it is grown. The lack of one fertilizing element or the excess of another can, without man's intervention, make the food unbalanced, dangerous in the long run or even unfit for eating. The consumers' preference for citrus fruits with orange or yellow skins makes them reject those with an unfamiliar green tint. There is, in fact, no good reason to discard them, since they are just as tasty and natural as the others: but the consumer usually associates the colour green with unripe fruit.

The manifestations of nature are many and varied and agricultural products are but one form. Nature is not good *per se*. At best it is indifferent to man; otherwise it is downright hostile. Man has been able to exist on the face of the earth because he has been able to acquire the knowledge needed to thwart this hostility, to increase nature's margin of tolerance and, sometimes, albeit rarely, to harmonize its needs with his for a while. This theme will be developed in the first section of this book.

In our own time, the myth of the natural tends to exploit the fiction of "the healthy savage", but in reality is nothing more than a form of commercialization. D'Elme (1973) has pointed out that producers have created needs, not in relation to man's welfare but to the market's welfare. The desire for the natural or "traditional", which is the outcome of too much living in cities, is part and parcel of this system of false services satisfying false needs. It is a form of exploitation of the naïvety of the average man whose critical faculties are in full retreat before the onslaughts of the mass media.

The aim of this book is to try and show the analogies that exist, at the nutritional level, between traditional and non-traditional foods. It also shows that agricultural or other techniques can often alter the composition of traditional foods and that technology is able to influence the nutritional values of non-traditional foods. The consumer should thus be in a better position to compare the two kinds of foods. Finally, the procedures established at the international level to protect the consumer are outlined by looking at the work of some international organizations that act as advisors to governments and whose recommendations are free from all outside influence.

Part One

TRADITIONAL FOODS

HARMFUL SUBSTANCES INTRINSIC
TO NATURAL FOODS

Introduction

For a variety of reasons, natural, or traditional, foods are often contrasted with other foods that are considered to be sophisticated. There is, however, no list of natural foods, nor is there even a definition of them, and it is very difficult to draw the dividing line between the two categories. If one decides that "natural" means that which is based on nature or, better still, which is imposed by nature, then there would appear to be an infinite variety of natural things. The composition of a foodstuff can vary considerably. This also holds true for meat: "There is no such thing as a meat; there are only meats [1]." Given such variety, how can one possibly select the truly natural product? How can one choose between wheat produced on land rich in selenium and wheat grown on normal land, which lacks this trace element — which of these wheats is natural? Both can be considered natural, but wheat produced both on land over-rich in selenium and on land completely lacking it can be harmful to the consumer.

The quality of naturalness, which in food is closely associated with the idea of what is considered traditional, already appears to be impossible to define. The same plant or the same animal, grown or reared in conditions that, while being completely natural, may vary considerably and reflect the influences of differing environments, will not, when growth is completed, always produce individuals that are exactly alike. The genotype's faculty of adaptation entails, for the phenotype, possibilities of variation that are often considerable. Differences in the composition of the final product, which may even include elements that are nutritionally doubtful, form part of these possibilities.

Among these, though they belong to quite another sector, one should mention the residues found in foods that are considered natural and that are produced according to the tenets of biological farming (which is another term that still has to be defined, since all farming is biological).

The harmful or antinutritive substances that are naturally present in foodstuffs have by no means all been identified. Traditional foods have

---

[1] Drieux, Ferrando and Jacquot (1962).

been studied systematically for too short a time for a sufficient number of results to be available. Certain illnesses, such as allergies, and the lack of tolerance to gluten (coeliac disease)[1] and to sugars, are well known. Nevertheless, preference has been given to studies on the biological effects of new methods of preparing and conserving food, the effects of additives and the qualities of new non-traditional products appearing on the market. This is perfectly understandable. One always tends to have confidence in the past. It is reassuring. Whatever has been used over generations is confidently accepted as being valid, if not actually perfect, on the basis of ancestral usage passed down from one generation to the next by word of mouth, and without the benefit of any systematic study. The approval that tradition confers avoids the need for such studies. However, people are suspicious of any change, even the simplest, as occurred in the introduction of food canning. It was a good idea to limit the spread of some of these novelties which often tended to be improvisations. Legislation always followed technology. It still does, but slowly. Lawmakers tend to be traditionalists by culture and training and are slow to adapt to industrial development. Nor do they always understand it. Although they sometimes seem far-seeing and progressive in laws dealing with sociological matters, they remain very ignorant of biology and traditional when it comes to ordinary, everyday things, food in particular. Thus one often finds that progressive ideas and nature-faddism go together. Of course, it is absolutely essential for man not to lose contact with nature, but nature-faddism and its excesses actually demonstrate that he is losing this contact because his conception of nature, based on myths and preconceived notions, has become partially, if not totally, erroneous.

Food allergies and intolerance to foods

A single food may cause different disorders in different people. Bleumink (1970) did an important study on these disorders. Sometimes, as well as gastrointestinal disorders, the symptoms of these cases manifest themselves in different ways, ranging from digestive intolerance, such as intolerance to various products (lactose, sucrose, gluten), to allergic reactions, with their great diversity. Such reactions can be mild or can lead to cases of anaphylaxis. Among other reactions, it is worth mentioning the relatively rare permanent food allergies, which are characterized by the appearance of typical symptoms each time a particular food is eaten, no matter how

---

[1] Dissanayade et al. (1973) extracted three fractions from peptic/tryptic chyme of gluten, two of which are toxic to people suffering from coeliac disease.

frequently. This type of allergy remains even when the food involved is eaten after a lapse of several years.

Atopic allergies, i.e., those characterized by a hereditary predisposition, which affect 4 to 5 percent of the population, are, for the most part, genetic in origin. Each case is individual and there is no general rule, just as in the case of drug addiction. Heredity can influence reactions to food just as it can alter reactions to medicines. The World Health Organization (1974) has drawn attention to this last point. Favism, or acute haemolytic anaemia brought on by eating broad beans, is caused by a lack of glucose-6-phosphate dehydrogenase (G6PD). The lack of this enzyme varies among ethnic groups. According to Bottini *et al.* (1971), certain allelomorphs, P^a and P^g, are responsible for this enzymatic anomaly. The inability to tolerate certain substances such as lactose (as mentioned earlier) is peculiar to non-European peoples. Eskimoes, both adults and children, cannot absorb more than a cup of milk daily; they also show an intolerance to sucrose. In some of them, the consumption of sweets brings on a severe attack of diarrhoea and an elevation in blood sugar level (Draper and Bergan, 1973).

It is not unusual, among breast-fed babies of a few months of age, to find a greater intolerance to protein in cow's milk; this can be acute or sub-acute, and occurs in around 7 percent of babies. In children, the signs of allergy to cow's milk vary widely. Goldman *et al.* (1963) gave a list of them and Gerrard *et al.* (1967) gave another. Bleumink (1970) compared the two lists in the table given on the following page.

While on the subject of milk and children, it is worth mentioning, in passing, that feeding children with cow's milk that is low in iron can encourage the deficiency of this element when the diet does not provide sufficient amounts from other sources.

Bleumink (1970) considers that there are also people who are allergic to tomatoes, oranges, bananas, nuts, chocolate, cereals, meat, and, much more rarely, to peas and spinach, and, more rarely still, to potatoes. Nearly all our foods, including strawberries, are mentioned. In the end, any of them can be responsible, to varying degrees, for cases of allergy. Some specialists think that allergies from eggs are rarer than those caused by bread, potatoes or even tomatoes. One trace element, manganese, which plays a useful role in metabolic reactions, can also cause allergy. According to Saakadze, Alekseeva and Mandzhgaladze (1973), men who work for a long time in magnesium mines become allergic to this trace element. The same phenomenon has also been observed in guinea-pigs.

There is general agreement, however, that one should classify cow's milk [1], along with eggs and fish, as one of the foods causing allergies.

---

[1] Often, however, there is confusion between an intolerance to lactose and an allergy to milk.

Symptom	Number of patients	
	Goldman *et al.* (1963)	Gerrard *et al.* (1967)
TOTAL no. of patients	89	150
Rhinitis	31	–
Rhinorrhoea	–	43
Asthma	24	26
Bronchitis	–	79
Atopic dermatitis	31	–
Eczema	–	20
Colic, abdominal pains	25	28
Vomiting	29	51
Diarrhoea	33	50
Diarrhoea with bleeding	–	20
Urticaria	10	–
Anaphylaxis	8	–

NOTE: Multiple and different symptoms may appear in the same child.

The substances that cause these reactions have been isolated. Milk β-lactoglobulin is among them, as well as ovalbumin in eggs, according to some authors.

It is worth stressing that, in the aetiology of these disorders, the effects of the soil of the food-production area (atopic allergies), storage (which can bring about the production of histamines in certain foods such as fish) and, finally, cooking should be taken into consideration. It is also clear, as Bleumink (1970) rightly stresses, that certain additives can also have an effect and thus should be controlled (as most countries now do) by observing the recommendations laid down by the Joint FAO/WHO Expert Committee on Food Additives.

However, all aspects should be given their due weight and one should not exaggerate the risks of additives that have been carefully evaluated beforehand. It was with the excesses of such exaggeration in mind, as well as food allergies, that the late Prof. A.C. Fraser remarked: "Just because some people are allergic to lobster doesn't mean that we have to limit its consumption!" This remark was both witty and wise. Regulations are only necessary when a large group of individuals is incurring risks from situations and conditions that are generalized. We cannot bring in regulations when only a few individuals are involved. The abuse of regulations is dangerous, because general control is impossible. It is a better policy to educate the consumer when the effects in question are marginal.

Ichthyotoxicity

Although an examination of classically toxic foods (such as mushrooms, which kill quite a large number of people every year) does not fall within the scope of this work, it will be useful quickly to review fish, shellfish and other animals living in fresh and salt water that, apart from their allergenic effects, can cause poisoning that is occasionally fatal. In 1969, Baslow devoted a study to this subject and in 1970, Cheymol spoke on the problem during a congress for the advancement of science. He referred to the puffer fish (*Arothron hispidus*) and especially to fish of the families and genera that cause ciguatera poisoning.

More recently, Ehrhardt (1971) drew attention to ichthyotoxins as a whole. Among fish alone there are more than 500 species that are dangerous to man. The dangerous toxins can be present in the blood, in the gonads, roe or milt, or in the flesh itself. They can also appear as a result of secondary bacterial contamination, which will not be considered here.

The isolation of ichthyotoxins and the elucidation of their structure are now under way. One of them, a fat-soluble toxin (ciguatoxin) [1], isolated from *Seriola aureovittata* by Hashimoto and Fusetani in 1968, has a LD_{50} of 20 $\mu g/g$ in the mouse.

The ecological aspect is already well understood, but it will take some time for the problem to be completely solved.

As regards ichthyism, one can divide fish into three groups: ichthyohaemotoxic, ichthyotoxic and ichthyosarcotoxic.

The first group includes the eel; the second includes sturgeon, salmon, pike and turbot; the third group is the largest, and includes the white and the red tunny, mackerel, mullet and fish that cause a severe type of ciguatera poisoning. Some toxins of this type, such as tetraodontoxin, are very frequently thermostable. Moreover, it is rare to see signs of poisoning in people who have eaten tunny, mackerel, mullet, etc. The Japanese call a neurotoxin of this type "fugu poison", which is sometimes used for criminal purposes.

According to several authors, the toxicity of the latter group of fish is due to the type of foods they eat. Some plankton, algae and corals appear to be toxiferous or toxigenic, not for the fish that consume them but, passed on by

---

[1] Ciguatoxin is accompanied by a water-soluble ciguaterin.

the fish, for the human consumer (Morelon and Niaussat, 1967). There exists, therefore, a true ecology of ichthyism, and Japanese investigators are making every effort to elucidate it. It could be that the situation is similar to that found in some shellfish that feed on dinoflagellate plankton, which produces a thermostable alkaloid. These dinoflagellates, such as *Gonyaulax catanella*, do not affect the living creature that absorbs them directly; however, in the human who absorbs them indirectly through eating shellfish, they produce severe poisoning that is sometimes fatal. Such poisonings have occurred in Canada, the United States and the United Kingdom.

Apart from the disorders caused by sea-urchins reported from Japan and Barbados (Feigen, Sanz and Alender, 1966), there have been poisonings resulting from the eating of mussels (*Mytilus edulis* and *M. californianus*), which were caused by mytilotoxin and mytilocongestin, isolated by Brieger (1889) and Richet (1907) respectively. The toxic material produced by *M. californianus* seems to be identical to that produced by *G. catanella*. The plankton (dinoflagellate) also confers its toxicity to *Saxidomus giganteus*, an Alaskan shellfish that contains saxitonin. However, some authorities think that there may be other toxic sources in the latter case.

Certain crabs can be poisonous, some during the reproductive cycle and others after feeding on gonyaulax.

In the work of Baslow (1969), 19 pages are devoted to a summary of the toxic and pharmacodynamic effects of substances isolated from diverse organisms living in fresh and salt water. The pharmacodynamic effects are not all harmful, as some of them (starting with those of sea-water itself) are antibacterial, amoebicidal, antiulcerative and stimulate growth of the reticulo-endothelial system. For fish alone, Wills (1966) gives a list of 98 that are reputed to be more or less toxic including, apart from those already mentioned, anchovies, herrings, conger eels, rays, cod, and perch.

Nature is thus not always perfect in the field of food (nor in other fields). As Truhaut (1966) has said, these problems must be clarified since one cannot forbid the consumption of several hundred species, which taste delicious, on the grounds that some individuals of these species are poisonous or have been known to be so in certain circumstances. He points out that this would ruin island economies that depend on the sea and, since both consumers and fishermen would start to avoid these (reportedly) poisonous species and concentrate on other species, they would destroy the equilibrium of the ichthyological fauna. He notes also that atolls and their lagoons seem to be the ideal environment for fish culture, which is now becoming an important aspect of the exploitation of the sea.

In view of the large amount of proteins that come from the sea, it is very important that we should carefully study the toxicity of foods that are of marine origin.

Present-day population growth obliges us to promote methods that depend for their development on a complete solution of the problems related to ichthyism, not to mention that other form of ichthyism that derives from pollution. A recent example of the latter was the Minamata disease, caused by eating fish from Minamata Bay, after the disposal of mercury into it and the transformation of the heavy metal into methyl mercury. In this case, one single factory was responsible and man's own carelessness, thus, was added to the complexities of nature.

The wholesomeness of food should never be neglected. It should have priority over everything, including the economy of a region or a country, since economic development depends on the health of the people.

Harmful glycosides

Plants and their various parts have numerous glycosides whose aglycone radical can have pharmacodynamic properties or be poisonous. For these properties to manifest themselves there has to be an initial hydrolysis. Usually this hydrolysis is due to an enzyme present in the part of the plant that is used. Preparatory grinding or cooking, or even the cooking process itself can be enough to produce this reaction. A light acid-hydrolysis can also be enough to cause the reaction. A typical example of this hydrolysis reaction is that seen in the lima bean (*Phaseolus lunatus*). A glycoside, linamarin, is hydrolysed under the action of a β-glucosidase producing glucose and 2-cyano-2-propanol, which, under the influence of an oxynitrilase, gives acetone and hydrocyanic acid, a well-known poison. During the First World War there were several cases of poisoning from eating lima beans. The first two studies on this form of hydrolysis were by Dunstan and Henry (1903) on *Phaseolus lunatus* and Bertrand (1906) on vetch seed (*Vicia sativa* var. *angustifolia*). Prolonged cooking can destroy the enzyme responsible for the hydrolysis but, at the symposium on legumes held in Rome in 1973, Liener (1973) reported that, according to Gabel and Kruger (1920), subjects who had eaten lima beans that had been carefully cooked to destroy the enzyme still eliminated HCN in their urine. It has been presumed, therefore, that certain enzymes in the digestive tract, or secreted by Enterobacteriaceae could also cause the hydrolysis of the cyanogenic glycoside. According to Winkler (1958) *Escherichia coli* could be one of these bacteria.

Certain bean varieties, such as those from Java, can give more than 300 mg of HCN per 100 g. It is very likely that farming methods can influence the production of the glycoside, as can be seen in the case of linseed where the level of linamaroside varies according to the country of origin of the seed.

TABLE 1. Principal glycosides present in human and animal foodstuffs

Glycoside	Source food	Hydrolysis products
Amygdalin and prunasin	Almonds and the kernels of dried shell fruit	Gentiobiose + HCN + benzaldehyde (the reaction can take place in two stages by the transformation of amygdalin into prunasin)
Linamaroside	Linseed and linseed cake	D-glucose + HCN + acetone
Vicianin	Vetch (*Vicia sativa* and *V. sativa* var. *angustifolia*	Vicianose + HCN + benzaldehyde
Linamarin (Paseolunatin)	Lima beans (*Phaseolus lunatus*)	D-glucose + HCN + acetone
–	Chickpeas and beans[1] (*Cicer arietinum* and *Vicia faba*)	HCN, but the reaction has not been verified and is perhaps doubtful or of little importance
Lotusin	Lotus (*Lotus arabicus*)	D-glucose + HCN + lotoflavin
Dhurrin	Sorghum and millet (young, as fodder)	D-glucose + HCN + hydroxybenzaldehyde
Sinigrin	Black mustard (*Brassica juncea*)	D-glucose + allylisothiocyanate + $KHSO_4$
Glucoropin (progiotrin)	Various crucifers	D-glucose + 5-vinyl-2-thiooxazolidone or goitrin + HSO_4
Glucobrassicin	Various crucifers (Brassicaceae)	Various thiocyano compounds

Sources: Liener (1966); Sapeika (1969); Gontzea, Ferrando and Sutzesco (1968).
[1] The ill effects resulting from favism are also well known; favism affects several peoples, mainly in Mediterranean countries, and is caused by an enzyme deficiency of hereditary origin.

The presence of these cyanogenetic glycosides is not limited to legumes alone (see Table 1).

There are other glycosides, such as the thioglucosides and the benzylthioglucosides, which, by similar mechanisms of an enzymatic nature, produce, during their hydrolysis, thiocyanates, isothiocyanates and benzyl cyanates that are poisonous and capable of antithyroid action. This action – one of the major effects of these compounds – will be examined by studying the hormonal and antihormonal properties of foodstuffs. Onions (Saghir, Cowan and Salji, 1966), watercress (to which are attributed abortogenic and aphrodisiac properties), legumes (groundnuts, soybeans), and

TABLE 2. Thiocyanate content of selected legumes

Item	SCN⁻ (in mg per 100 g of fresh edible product)
Brassica oleracea var. *capitata* (cabbage)	3-6
B. ol. var. *sabauda* (savoy cabbage)	18-31
B. ol. var. *gemmifera* (Brussels sprouts)	10
B. ol. var. *botrytis* (broccoli, cauliflower)	4-10
B. ol. var. *gongyloides* (kohlrabi)	2-3
Brassica napus (colza, rape)	2.5
B. napus var. *rapifera* (swede)	9
Lettuce, spinach, onions, celery roots and leaves, haricot beans, radishes, tomatoes	Less than 1 mg, and often less than 0.5 mg

Sources: Gmelin and Virtanen (1959-60); Michajlowskiy and Langer (1958-59).

especially plants of the Cruciferae family contain these glycosides. It should, however, be noted that, according to Van der Velden *et al.* (1973), thiocyanates can be formed in rats starting from the cyanogenetic glucosides of cassava. Feeding rats with this food increases their plasma thiocyanate level. This level rises from 5 mg/l to 8.8 mg/l. This is the equivalent of around 1 mg of thiocyanate being eaten by the control group. The daily consumption of 10 g of cassava root containing 1.6 mg of HCN would be the equivalent of eating 1 to 2 mg of thiocyanate. The list of the main glycosides likely to be present in the more common foods is given in Table 1. This list will be completed to include goitrogenic compounds when they are discussed later (pages 48-51).

This partial information is completed by the data given in Table 2, which was derived from various sources and has been published before in Gontzea, Ferrando and Sutzesco (1968).

As regards food for humans, therefore, haricot beans and plants of the Cruciferae family contain variably toxic glycosides and preformed thiocyanates. One can understand, thus, the serious consequences caused by ingesting cyanogenetic glycosides. The endocrinal effects of sulphur-containing glycosides that are goitrogenic will be examined later. Finally, mention should be made of the glycoside of *Solanum malacoxylon*, which, on hydrolysis, produces 1,25-dihydroxycholecalciferol, the active metabolite of Vitamin D_3.

Toxic amino acids

The importance and biological role of the amino acids present in protein are well known. Ten of them are considered to be essential and should normally be present in the daily diet in sufficient quantities and in certain ratios to each other. But even these amino acids, although they are considered essential, can, in certain cases, also be toxic. Methionine, for example, if taken in excessive quantities can cause serious disorders [1]. According to Benevenga (1973, 1974), these disorders are due to faulty metabolism of the $- CH_3$ group and not to an effect on the transport of the other amino acids. The toxic product could be an intermediate compound that plays a role in breaking down methionine. There would appear to be three mechanisms in operation and these differ according to the concentration of methionine in the system. Longton (1973) has also shown that daily cutaneous application or intraperitoneal injection of amino acids causes lesions to the skin or internal organs of laboratory animals. The mechanism of these effects is unknown but the structure of the amino acids appears to play an important role. For example, *L*-aspartic acid is highly irritating to rabbit skin while *L*-glutamic acid is less active. *D*-aspartic acid and *D*-glutamic acid are less harmful. Pathological changes have been observed on internal organs after intraperitoneal injections of *L*-tyrosine, β-alanine and *L*-histidine. Such observations should be a warning to all those studying the toxicity of new compounds, and to those who sometimes go to any lengths to use surprising methods of introducing the product into experimental animals.

Apart from amino acids that are essential for the maintenance and perpetuation of life, and that may be toxic under certain conditions, there are others that our organism is able to synthesize, but which are equally toxic. Murti and Seshadri (1967), and then Thompson, Clayton and Smith (1969) have produced detailed and extremely interesting reports on these amino acids. However, only the main facts as they regard food will be examined here.

Lathyrism, which is associated with the eating of plants of the genus *Lathyrus*, is caused by β-amino-propionitrile, which is usually found in

---

[1] This is a basic research finding. In practice, the unpleasant taste imparted to food by an excess of *DL*-methionine ensures that a toxic dose is never ingested.

plants in the form of β-(N-γ-glutamyl)-amino-propionitrile and β-amino-propionitrile found in *Lathyrus odoratus, pusillus* and *hirsutus*, the causative agents of human lathyrism. Only the latter of the two compounds causes the bony lesions of osteo-lathyrism in the rat. The causative agent of human neurolathyrism has been isolated from *Lathyrus sativus*; it is β-N-oxalyl-α,β-diamino-propionic acid, which also causes severe neuro-logical symptoms in chickens, rats and monkeys when injected. Rao, Mala-thi and Sarma (1969) have examined this question.

These different toxic compounds can be classified as follows:

osteolathyrogenic β-amino-propionitrile and β-(N-γ-glutamyl)-amino-propionitrile	*Lathyrus odoratus* *L. pusillus* *L. hirsutus*
neurolathyrogenic α,γ-diamino-butyric acid	*L. latifolius* *L. sylvestris*
β-cyano-*L*-alanine	*L. sativus*
β-N-oxalyl-α,β-diamino-propionic acid	*L. sativus* *L. cicera* *L. clymenum*

According to Jeswani, Lal and Prakash (1970), it is possible to cultivate varieties of *Lathyrus* that do not contain these neurotoxic amino acids or that contain them in very small amounts. However, according to Liener (1973) these new varieties could contain other substances that are neuro-toxic.

The fruit of the ackee, *Blighia sapida*, found in Jamaica and Nigeria, contains α-amino-β-cyclopropanylpropionic acid, which has been studied by Hassal, Reyle and Feng (1954) and by De Renzo *et al.* (1959). This compound, hypoglycin A, is accompanied by hypoglycin B, a dipeptide. The pharmacological study of hypoglycins has been carried out by Chen, Fleming and Lin (1961). Hypoglycins cause an acute poisoning called "vomiting sickness" that can be fatal. A diet that is rich in carbohydrates increases the toxicity of the fruit, as Quevauviller (1974) has pointed out, citing the work of Feng and Kean (1955). The two compounds are also teratogenic. They seem to be competitive inhibitors of various hepatic enzymes, particularly *L*-leucine transaminase.

Mimosine inhibits the growth of wool in sheep and can even cause death.

It also inhibits the growth rate of rats and mice. But the plant that contains it (*Leucaena glauca*) is eaten by man and can be poisonous. Mimosine is an antagonist of tyrosine with which it bears a structural analogy (see figure below), but it could also be an antagonist of phenylalanine. Vitamin B_6 would also seem to counteract, in part, the harmful effects of mimosine.

$O=$ ⬡ $N-CH_2-CH-COOH$ HO ⬡ $CH_2-CH-COOH$
$\quad\quad\quad\quad\quad\quad\quad\quad\quad | \quad\quad\quad\quad\quad\quad\quad\quad\quad\quad\quad\quad\quad\quad\quad\quad\quad |$
$OH\quad\quad\quad\quad\quad\quad\quad\quad NH_2\quad\quad\quad\quad\quad\quad\quad\quad\quad\quad\quad\quad\quad\quad\quad NH_2$

Mimosine   Tyrosine

The structures of mimosine and tyrosine

Canavanine, which has a very rare chemical group in its molecule, is found in soybeans, certain haricot beans and in 17 types of vetch. Canavanine is also an antagonist of an essential amino acid: arginine. A reference should also be made to djenkolic acid, the structure of which is close to that of cystine but for which it is neither a substitute nor an antagonist. "Djenko sickness" is a disorder of the urinary tract that afflicts exotic-food fans who eat the djenko bean (*Pithecolobium lobatum*). As Van Veen points out (1966), there can be from 1 to 2 percent of djenkolic acid in the plant, and even as much as 3 to 4 percent in the black variety. Disorders only occur if the consumer's urine has an acid reaction that allows the compound to precipitate in the form of fine needles that cause lesions. To protect themselves, those who eat these beans also consume the alkaline extract of ash of various plants.

$S-CH_2-CH-COOH$ $S-CH_2-CH-COOH$
$|\quad\quad\quad\quad |\quad\quad\quad\quad\quad\quad\quad\quad\quad |\quad\quad\quad\quad\quad\quad |$
$CH_2\quad\quad NH_2\quad\quad\quad\quad\quad\quad\quad\quad\quad\quad\quad\quad NH_2$
$|\quad\quad\quad\quad\quad\quad\quad\quad\quad\quad\quad\quad\quad\quad |$
$\quad\quad NH_2\quad\quad\quad\quad\quad\quad\quad\quad\quad\quad\quad\quad NH_2$
$|\quad\quad\quad\quad |\quad\quad\quad\quad\quad\quad\quad\quad\quad |\quad\quad\quad\quad\quad\quad |$
$S-CH_2-CH-COOH$ $S-CH_2-CH-COOH$

Djenkolic acid   Cystine

Some of the sulphur-containing amino acids, such as allicin, derived from two alliin molecules and extracted from garlic, would seem to be beneficial, thanks to their antibacterial and fungicidal properties, and may even sometimes be anti-tumoral[1] but, unfortunately, they are also anti-enzymat-ic and it is this property that has probably been the cause of some disorders in young children.

$$2\begin{cases} CH_2-CH=CH_2 \\ | \\ S\ldots O \qquad NH_2 \\ | \qquad\quad | \\ CH_2-CH-COOH \end{cases} \xrightarrow[H_2O]{Alliinase} \begin{array}{l} S-CH_2-CH=CH_2 \\ | \\ O \\ | \\ S-CH_2-CH=CH_2 \end{array} + 2\ CH_3-CO-COOH + 2\ NH_3$$

Alliin	Allicin + pyruvic acid
$C_6H_{11}O_3NS$	$(C_3H_5S)_2O$

Generally speaking, distrust, an awareness of dangers, and tradition keep people away from items that can hardly not be called real foods — especially when one considers the legumes previously referred to that are currently used in the diet and that sometimes unsuspectedly inconvenience or upset the metabolism, without any danger being suspected. Furthermore, in many countries consumers have no choice, since they must either take the risk or go hungry.

It is worth drawing the attention of exotic-food fans (another group of natural food faddists engendered by easy travel) to the risks they run in the "lands of their dreams" when they eat foods about whose potential harmfulness they know little or nothing.

The following sections cover substances contained in foods that are in more current use but that are capable of causing disorders, particularly when they are eaten during the course of certain types of therapy.

Amines

Basic analytical research data show that many foods in their natural state contain numerous amines, many of which are called biogenic amines because, in very small doses, they play a biological role (Täufel, 1970). They can modify certain cellular functions (e.g., of the nerve cells in the case of serotonin), intervene as the precursors of hormones, act as vasodilators and stimulants of gastric secretion (histamine) and enter into the structure of coenzymes. Nevertheless, even though, in normal conditions, these sub-

---

[1] Garlic seems to lower the blood cholesterol level (Jain, 1975).

TABLE 3. Amine content of selected fruits and legumes
(mg/100 g of fresh fruit)

	Serotonin	Tyramine	Dopamine	Noradrenalin
Banana (skin)	5-15	6.5	70	12.2
Banana (pulp)	2.8	0.7	0.8	0.2
Banana (pulp)	2-10	–	–	0.2
Pineapple (ripe)	2	–	–	
Pineapple (juice)	2.5-3.5	–	–	–
Avocado	1	2.3	5	0
Passion-fruit	0.1-0.4	–	–	–
Tomato	1.2	0.4	0	0
Red plum	1	0.6	0	+
Dark plum	0	–	–	0
Eggplant	0.2	0.3	0	0
Potato	0	0.1	0	0.2
Orange	0	1.0	0	+

Source: Sapeika (1969).
According to Liew and Chang (1972), bananas from Malaysia contain 5-hydroxytryptamine at the level of 4-140 μ/g in the skin and 35-140 μg/g in the pulp. The amount decreases with ripening.

stances may not be harmful, they can, in some sensitive subjects, have harmful effects that are all the more marked when, as mentioned earlier, they interfere with the effect of medicaments. This whole question has been reviewed by Lovenberg (1974).

When the data shown in Table 3 are considered, it may seem astonishing that these amines can reach such high levels in some common fruits and particularly in some tropical fruits such as the banana.

According to Mayer, Pause and Vetsch (1973), most sauerkraut that is sold also contains non-volatile biogenic amines that are active or toxic. The methods of preparation and the action of the anaerobic flora on the production of 2-phenylethylamine, isoamylamine, tyramine, ethanolamine, cadaverine, putrescine and histamine have been well studied. It is now possible to produce sauerkraut with low levels of histamine and tyramine by inhibiting the growth of certain bacteria (*Pediococci*).

According to Wang (1972), soybeans or soy flour that have not been defatted contain 29 µg/g of polyamines.

Growing conditions can also influence the levels of these amines since, according to Smith (1973), the leaves of barley grown on land lacking in potassium contain 13.3 times more putrescine than barley grown on land rich in this mineral element; in plants lacking in magnesium, the level of putrescine is 3.8 times higher, while the lack of phosphorus or nitrogen reduces the level of putrescine. Of course there are optimum methods of fertilization that can alter the quantities of biogenic amines in plants as they can for the other constituent elements of these plants, particularly the proteins, vitamins and trace elements.

Other foods that come from the processing of products of animal or vegetable origin also contain amines.

High levels of amines are found in cheeses, according to reports in various publications such as those of the Food Protection Committee (USA) or, more recently, those published by Spettoli (1971a and b). This can be seen from a selection of figures taken from various publications relating to an international sampling of some excellent cheeses.

Cheese	Amine	Amount found (µ/100 g)
Camembert	Tyramine	90-200
Camembert	Histamine	209-255
Camembert	Putrescine	92-143
Emmenthaler	Tyramine	0-50
Emmenthaler	Histamine	65-240
English Cheddar	Tyramine	72-332
Gorgonzola	Tyramine	158-167
Parmesan	Tyramine	20-28
Gouda	Tyramine	0-50
Gouda	Histamine	65-240
Gouda	Tryptamine	40-96

Still in the cheese sector, Freimuth and Gläser also found (1970) dimethylnitrosamine (120 µg/kg) and traces of diethylnitrosamine. These compounds will be considered later.

Kurisaki *et al.* (1973) found from 1 to 20 µg/g of benzoic acid in 25 types of cheese they examined. The benzoic acid could come from the breakdown of hippuric acid, as the authors have shown experimentally. These levels are low compared with the acceptable daily intake, which is around 10 mg/kg of body weight/day. It is to be noted that honey and certain berries also contain benzoic acid.

Some of these cheeses also contain moulds that give them an extremely agreeable flavour. In one of these, *Penicillium roqueforti*, Kanota (1970) identified three metabolites, two of which are toxic when isolated from their complex with the food and, especially, when they are extracted from the surface of the cultures, but not from the mycelium.

It is not only cheese that contains amines. Wine, which, from the gastronomical point of view, goes so well with cheese, also contains them. Certain red wines and grapes contain polyphenol-type compounds that, according to Masquelier (1959), have an antibiotic action in the digestive tract and are capable of acting synergistically with antibiotics; these same red wines may also contain from 5 to 20 mg of histamine per litre (Marquardt, Schmidt and Spath, 1963). Pyrrolidine is also present and, in 1971, Spettoli found such amines as ethylamine, isobutylamine, tyramine, ethanolamine and histamine in Italian wines. The figures given by this author are lower than those found by German researchers. The average found for the 10 wines examined was 2.05 mg/l. Chianti had a total of only 1.90 mg/l of amines while a 1964 pinot broke all records with 2.53 mg/l. Plumas (1971) also examined this question. Ayhan and Kayaalp (1971) showed that the introduction of acidified beer into the stomachs of cats that have been given a monoamine oxidase inhibitor causes their blood pressure to rise. Alkaline solutions of beer are inactive in the absence of the drug. Beer, like wine, therefore, may also contain amines produced during the fermentation process. The dangers that these amines present to consumers will be examined later. First, it is worth noting that in addition to the amines present in our natural food and drink there are also those resulting from the microbial breakdown that takes place in the digestive tract. The amount of these is often significant. They are all, however, neutralized, particularly by the formation of corresponding non-toxic compounds, the carboxylic acids, under the influence of the enzyme monoamine oxidase. The foods mentioned above may, however, have untoward effects similar to those found in cats by Ayhan and Kayaalp (1971) on consumers who are being treated with medicines that inhibit monoamine oxidase. The inhibition of monoamine oxidase, which normally neutralizes the amines in these foods, leads to strong hypertension, fierce headaches and sometimes even to cerebral haemorrhage (Perrault, 1965).

It is also known that some populations in which there is a high rate of banana consumption can absorb up to 200 mg per day of serotonin, an amine that causes the cardiac lesions of myocardial fibrosis. Finally, it should be mentioned that the unpleasant effects caused by the amines in food may be more acute in those who suffer from hyperthyroidism. Experiments show that thyroxine seems to increase the effects of amines in mice. Although it is in a different form, this brings us back to phenomena similar to those previously mentioned, those resulting from interferences between the lack, or a low level, of iodine and the ingestion of foods containing antithyroids. Such findings should encourage us to consider these questions as a whole and, especially, never to forget the close but frequently overlooked links that exist between food, illness and therapy. The association of the natural antinutritive or pharmacodynamically active substances in foods with certain medicines can be just as dangerous as the use of two antagonistic medicines. While such a study is beyond the scope of the present work this still demonstrates that the consumer remains closely linked to what he eats at every moment and in every circumstance of his life.

Nitrosamines

Nitrosamines are chemical compounds formed by the action of nitrous acid on a secondary amine. This reaction has been known for a long time. Nitrates are widespread in nature. They are found in all plants, and some vegetables (spinach, celery, green salads, etc.) contain appreciable amounts. Certain circumstances can favour their accumulation, e.g., absence of molybdenum. Lacassagne (1967) notes a report by Burrell, Roach and Schadwell (1966) who, while surveying the Transkei, noticed that cancer of the oesophagus had become quite frequent when, 25 years previously, it had been unknown. There were "cancer gardens" and gardens whose owners were not affected. The women were more sedentary than the men (who emigrated for work for part of each year) and were the most frequently affected. Burrell, Roach and Schadwell (1966) recognized that in most of these "cancer gardens" the soil was lacking in molybdenum. This trace element is needed to metabolize the nitrates in plants. Its absence prevents the transformation of nitrates into ammonia and favours the production of nitrosamines.

Excessive use of nitrate fertilizer gives the same effect, which is cumulative in the absence of molybdenum, but less marked in its presence. It should be noted that the use of nitrates also interacts with the variety of plant considered.

In a study carried out on 95 samples of potatoes taken from different US markets, Heisler, Cording and Aceto (1973) found an average of 120 μg/g of nitrates and 0.44 μg/g of nitrites. In all the samples there was a positive correlation between the level of nitrates and that of nitrites. The level of nitrates depends only slightly on fertilization, as the following figures taken from Heisler, Cording and Aceto show:

Manure				NO$_3$ (according to variety of potato)		
Dunging	N	P$_2$O$_5$	K$_2$O	Saskia	Krasava	Blanik
....	kg/ha	....		....	mg/kg	....
0	0	0	0	122.7	123.7	67.2
250	0	0	0	133.2	124.8	80.0
250	40	40	80	134.5	116.7	94.7
250	80	40	80	125.7	152.0	84.5
250	120	40	80	196.8	190.5	106.8

There are thus many factors governing the level of nitrates in food and hence, indirectly, the formation of nitrosamines.

The method of preparation of food can also have an influence. The exposure of foods rich in nitrates to damp heat for some time encourages the reduction of nitrates to nitrites, due to the action of bacteria that are always present. This is why nitrites are formed in soups rich in carrots, which always contain nitrates (L'Hirondelle et al., 1971). Soup should neither be kept for a long time nor re-heated: "A re-heated dinner is worthless," wrote Boileau . . . even from the point of view of hygiene.

Amines exist in many foods in the natural state (see above) and the cooking of foods rich in protein can also release free amino acids such as proline and hydroxyproline that can nitrosate at 35-40°C in a slightly acidic medium. Nitrosoproline can change into nitrosopyrrolidine, a nitrosamine.

Wolff and Wasserman (1972) stress the fact that the N-nitrosamines are carcinogenic and may also be mutagenic and teratogenic. Of the approximately 100 compounds they examined, 75 caused lesions in experimental animals. N-nitrosodimethylamine appears to be carcinogenic in the rat at doses above 5 μg/g. The compound is present in a great many foods and it can also develop as a result of the interaction of various elements, as we shall see later on.

Lijinsky (1970, 1972) stressed that nitrosamines can also develop from nitrites and from medicines such as oxytetracycline, aminopyrine, disulfiram and tolazamide. The reaction between aminopyrine and oxytetracycline causes the formation of considerable amounts of dimethylnitrosamine. However, the physico-chemical conditions of the environment play an important role, which we shall return to later on.

Referring only to foods (and apart from those mentioned in connection with amines), hung meat, stale fish and some cheeses (see page 17) contain diamines such as cadaverine and putrescine, as well as dimethylnitrosamine and diethylnitrosamine. Dimethylamine and diethylamine are also found in cereals, tea and soybeans. Finally, during alcoholic fermentation pyrrolidine is formed as well as the group of amines listed as being present in wine (p. 18).

Secondary, tertiary and quaternary amines in food react with nitrites to form nitrosamines under the influence of bacteria or under certain physico-chemical conditions (i.e., of pH) comparable with those found in the stomach during the secretion of gastric juice. According to Mirvish (1971) this is how the nitrosation of a compound such as methylguanidine, or amino acids such as arginine and citruline, takes place. According to Wolff and Wasserman (1972) the thiocyanates present in human saliva (12-33 mg/100 ml), especially in that of smokers, promote the reaction of nitrosation.

Sen et al. (1973) noted that a mixture of black pepper, paprika, two other spices and 0.96 percent of sodium nitrite leads to the formation of nitrosopyrrolidine. It appears that some amines in the spices − piperidine and pyrrolidine, for example − react with sodium nitrite to form nitrosamines. Black pepper and paprika would thus promote the formation of nitrosopiperidine, while black pepper leads especially to the production of nitrosopyrrolidine and paprika to that of nitrosopiperidine. N-nitrosodimethylamine has also been detected after interaction between paprika and sodium nitrite [1].

It is also worth noting that, in an acid environment, tannins have a very marked inhibiting effect on the reaction between dimethylamine and diethylamine, on the one hand, and nitrites on the other. The tannin and amines seem to be in competition with the nitrites (Bogovski et al., 1972).

Several researchers, including Sander and Schweinsberg (1973) and Sen et al. (1973), achieved the formation of compounds such as diethylnitrosamine by the incubation of diethylamine in the presence of nitrites in gastric juice taken from man, rats, rabbits, dogs and cats. The formation of nitrosamines could be induced by this mechanism. Intestinal bacteria, particularly several strains of Escherichia coli and other microorganisms isolated by Hawksworth and Hill (1971) from the digestive tract of humans, are capable of nitrosating amines at a neutral pH. This phenomenon could also take place in the bladder of people with urinary infections. Some authors point

---

[1] Red pepper given to rats over a year and a half increased the incidence of liver tumours caused by the carcinogen p-dimethyl-amino-azobenzene.

out that 90 percent of these infections are due to *E. coli*, whose capacity for nitrosation has been mentioned.

It should also be noted that, in experiments using laboratory animals, nitrosamines have caused serious liver lesions and sometimes even malignant liver tumours with metastases. Tumours of the lung have also been caused in experiments with dimethylnitrosamine, dinitropiperazine, nitrosomorpholine and *N*-nitro-*N*-methylamine (Greenblatt, Mirvish and So Bing, 1971).

Thus, the nitrosamines formed from the compounds present in food or supplied by medicines could be a potential source of carcinogenesis.

We are only beginning to discover the amount of amines in our daily foods. There have been few studies on the subject since, up to now, the traditional foods have not attracted much attention. Even when vegetable produce is grown on land with little or no application of nitrate fertilizer, it still contains nitrates. In any case, sodium nitrite has been used for a long time in the curing of meat and pork. Studies carried out in the Federal Republic of Germany have shown that the average person consumes 1.5 mg of pure nitrite each day, mainly from meat sources. For Keybets, Groot and Keller (1970) the safe limit is 0.1 mg/kg of body weight. Tests by these authors on spinach have shown that it contains less than 0.08 mg/kg of diethylnitrosamine, even though spinach is considered as being particularly liable to store nitrates. To this, however, must be added other "natural" sources of amines as well as those resulting from the reaction of enterobacteria.

It would be most desirable, therefore, to forbid the use of nitrites, but such a step would also have serious drawbacks from the point of view of hygiene. There have recently been some disputes on this question. Lijinsky (1973) states that some people have exaggerated the dangers of nitrites in the aetiology of cancer. In his view, the protection of the consumer against botulism is much more important. He considers that experiments made in the space of two years with 150 animals cannot be set against the fact that millions of people have been consuming nitrites for more than 50 years. Moreover, a technical note printed in 1973 stated that the addition of sodium ascorbate or sodium erythorbate prevents the formation of nitrosamines [1] in frankfurters. Finally, Fazio *et al.* (1973) noted that *N*-nitrosopyrrolidine is found in cooked bacon, in amounts of between 10 and 118 µg/kg; it is not found in raw bacon. Cooking, therefore, has an effect on its formation.

---

[1] This action of ascorbic acid and its salts has since been confirmed. However, some countries seem to be tending toward the prohibition of nitrites.

It should also be noted that small amounts of nitrosamines are found in tobacco and that it would be wise to forbid its use; but this would no doubt be difficult to achieve.

Of course, all amines are not liable to give rise to nitrosamines and all of the latter are certainly not carcinogenic. But we do know of 75 that seem to be so. This complex problem should be studied very carefully and we should ask ourselves some basic questions about the foods we consume every day, even though they do not contain any substances other than those which exist naturally or are liable to form naturally.

Anti-enzymes, haemagglutinins and substances causing flatulence

A large part of a publication by Gontzea, Ferrando and Sutzesco (1968) was devoted to the study of the inhibitors of digestive enzymes present in various common foods. These inhibitors, found in foodstuffs of vegetable and animal origin, not only reduce (sometimes by a considerable extent) the digestive utilization of food proteins, but also those supplied by other components of the diet.

Osborn and Mendel (1912) were the first to notice that in order to achieve normal growth in a rat fed on soybeans, it helped if the grain was heated beforehand. In 1945, Kunitz isolated from raw soybeans a globulin with a high molecular weight that can combine with trypsin to form a compound without any enzymatic action. Since then there have been many studies carried out on such antitryptic factors.

Among the foods of animal origin containing this antitryptic property one should mention raw egg-white and colostrum. Delezenne and Pozersky first pointed it out for raw egg-white in 1903. Later a polypeptide was isolated that could slow down and reduce the normal release of amino acids in food, particularly lysine, threonine and valine, thus causing a reduction of at least 10 percent in the digestive utilization coefficient (DUC) of nitrogen. This antitryptic factor is resistant to drying but is destroyed in cooking.

While on the subject of eggs, it is worth registering a protest against the over-frequent accusations made against this excellent food in connection with hypercholesterolaemia. Pope (1971) has pointed out that one egg gives 240 mg of cholesterol while a healthy person produces between 1 500 and 2 000 mg per day. It is also possible to produce eggs that are rich in linoleic acid and thus indirectly lower the blood cholesterol level of the consumer.

In the case of colostrum, which is secreted in the first few days of lacta-tion, the presence of an anti-enzyme would seem to be beneficial. During the first few hours of life of an infant, some substances that are present in the colostrum and that play a role in establishing immunity in the newborn child need a highly permeable intestinal mucosa and should not be subject to alterations by the digestive process. For this purpose they are protected by an anti-enzyme that counteracts the trypsin of the pancreas. This anti-enzyme is found in women, cows and sows. According to Laskowki *et al.* (referred to in Gontzea, Ferrando and Sutzesco, 1968), 1 ml of sow colostrum inhibits the action of 2 000 μg of crystallized trypsin. Cow colostrum inhibits 600 μg, and that taken from 10 women who had just given birth inhibited 60 μg at the most.

A similar antitrypsin seems to exist also in raw milk, but in lower quantities. All these anti-enzymes are rendered inactive by prolonged, moist heat. The pasteurization process (heating at 72°C for 40 seconds) only reduces the antitrypsin action by between 3 and 4 percent. Even when boiled for a short time, the milk still retains its trypsin-inhibiting factor. The inhibitors are found mainly in the lipid components of colostrum and milk (Taranov and Vladimirov, 1971).

TABLE 4. Enzyme inhibitors in selected products, excluding leguminous seeds

Product	Enzyme inhibited	Reference
Alfalfa	Trypsin	Ramirez and Mitchell, 1960
Wheat	Trypsin	Gontzea *et al.*, 1956-57 [1]
Flour (of wheat, rice, oats, maize, barley, rye, buckwheat)	Trypsin, chymotrypsin	Laporte and Trémolières, 1962
Rice	Trypsin	Polanowski, 1967
Maize	Trypsin	Hochstrasser, Muss and Werle, 1967
Barley	Trypsin	Mikola and Snolinna, 1969
Potatoes	Protease	Bessmo and Kurosawa, 1967
Potatoes	Trypsin, chymotrypsin	Santarius and Belitz, 1972
Potatoes	Trypsin, chymotrypsin	Worowski and Fabiszewski, 1973
Guar flour (*Cyamopsis tetragonoloba*)	Trypsin	Couch, Creger and Bakshi, 1966
Cuttlefish liver solubles	Trypsin	Ishikawa *et al.*, 1966

Note: Most of these anti-enzymes are thermolabile.
[1] See Gontzea, Ferrando and Sutzesco (1968).

Foods of vegetable origin contain numerous enzyme inhibitors. Santarius and Belitz (1972) isolated two different inhibitors, one of trypsin and another of chymotrypsin, in potatoes. Recently a substance has even been discovered (in the crust of loaves of bread) that inhibits the digestion of starch.

Amylases have been noted in certain beans (Jaffe and Vega, 1968), but they are destroyed by heat. Gontzea, Ferrando and Sutzesco (1968) showed between 1956 and 1957 that wheat contains antitrypsins.

These antitrypsins are mostly found in leguminous seeds, particularly in those of the soybean as well as of various other types of bean. Beans are one of the most widely eaten foods in the world, particularly by the peoples of Latin America and parts of Africa and India. Apart from these antitrypsin factors, these leguminous seeds contain haemagglutinins and substances that cause flatulence. It has already been described how certain grains can contain glycosides and harmful amino acids. It will be shown later that they may also have antihormonal properties.

Although the presence of enzyme inhibitors is not limited to leguminous seeds only − they are found in alfalfa, guar, cereals (wheat and rice) and in potatoes (see Table 4) − it is clear that the question of anti-enzymes is of the utmost importance in the case of leguminous seeds. For this reason the subject will be examined here; for greater detail, reference should be made to the works already mentioned and to the extensive report (published in 1973) on the meeting on leguminous plants held in Rome in 1972 by the Protein-Calorie Advisory Group (PAG) of the United Nations [1].

The biological significance of these anti-enzymes is uncertain. Some authors suggest they are a defence mechanism and a way of protecting certain compounds and their specific structures by inhibiting the degradation of the nitrogenous parts, which are of a protein nature. This hypothesis of a protective role seems to be justified when one considers the fact that the most active enzyme-inhibitors are found in those parts containing the reproductive elements of the egg or seed. Their level usually diminishes during the course of germination (Polanowski, 1967).

Gontzea, Ferrando and Sutzesco (1968) have shown this for wheat. In this connection, PAG Report No. 22 cites the work of Birk, Gertler and Kholz (1963); Lipke, Fraenkel and Liener (1954); and, finally, Guen and Ryan (1972). The anti-enzyme activity could be a defence against insects and, according to Halim et al. (1973), against moulds (at least for maize, which

---

[1] In January 1978, PAG was replaced by a new institutional body consisting of a Sub-Committee on Nutrition (SCN) of the UN Administrative Coordination Committee with the technical support of the Advisory Group on Nutrition (AGN).

TABLE 5. Performance of rats receiving a diet containing 40 percent bean flour and 0.3 percent *DL*-methionine

Diet	Weight gain or loss (g/day)
Uncooked red beans	[1] − 2.1
Uncooked red beans + digested casein ("casitone")	[1] − 1.8
Red beans cooked for two hours at 85°C	− 0.5
Red beans pressure-cooked at 118°C for 30 min	+ 2.8
Red beans pressure-cooked at 118°C for 30 min without added methionine	+ 0.4
Untreated white beans	+ 0.1
White beans + "casitone"	+ 2.3
White beans cooked for two hours at 85°C	+ 1.5
White beans pressure-cooked at 118°C for 30 min	+ 2.4
White beans pressure-cooked at 118°C for 30 min, without added methionine	+ 0.3

[1] All animals died in 10-14 days.

would thus be protected against the attacks of *Fusarium roseum* and, to a lesser degree, against *Helminthosporium maydis*). The elimination of this property through the selection and breeding of plants lacking it would doubtless cause serious storage problems. The antitrypsins are unquestionably less dangerous than is the casual use of certain pesticides. The ways of eliminating antitrypsins will be examined later.

The antinutritive activity of leguminous seeds, caused by enzyme inhibitors that can act jointly with other substances, is shown clearly in Table 5 (taken from Jaffe, 1973). The differences that exist between the two varieties of beans can be seen.

The favourable effects resulting from heat treatment and the addition of methionine are also found with soybeans, as is shown by the figures in Table 6 (taken from Liener, Devel and Fevold, 1949), and mentioned in the previously cited report of the PAG meeting (1973).

An even more detailed analysis, carried out by Kakade and Evans in 1966, shows that, when rats are fed raw *Phaseolus vulgaris* in a 10-percent

TABLE 6. Effect of heat and of methionine on the nutritive value of soybeans in the rat

Diet	Protein efficiency ratio
Uncooked soybean flour	1.33
Pressure-cooked soybean flour	2.62
Uncooked soybean flour + 0.6% of methionine	2.42

protein diet, they absorb less nitrogen and less of the amino acids methionine, cystine, lysine, leucine and valine than when the beans have been previously cooked in a pressure cooker.

The action of haemagglutinins adds to that of anti-enzymes. These proteins, called phytoagglutinins by Jaffe (1973) (also called lectins), were discovered in 1953. It has been estimated that these substances contribute some 25 percent to the growth inhibition caused by raw soybeans in the rat (see Table 7, taken from Liener, who did a general study on this question in 1974).

TABLE 7. Inhibitory action of phytohaemagglutinins of soybeans on the growth of rats

Source of protein in diet	Weight gain in two weeks (*grams*)	Growth inhibition (%)
25% of heated soybean flour	60	0
25% of uncooked soybean flour	28	43
25% of heated soybean flour + 0.8% of soybean haemagglutinins	45	26

In one of their papers (1973) Kakade *et al.* only attribute to antitryptic action 40 percent of the total depressant effect of soybeans and their action on the pancreas.

The haemagglutinating effect is found in various beans, and this changes according to the variety. Jaffe and Brucher (1972) developed a method to identify the different haemagglutinins of various types of bean. The following is a list, according to Liener (1974), of the species most commonly studied for haemagglutinins along with their molecular weights.

Species	Molecular weight of haemagglutinin
Jack bean (*Canavalia ensiformis*)	112 000
Soybean (*Glycine max*)	110 000
Lentil (*Lens esculenta*)	42 000-69 000
Lima bean (*Phaseolus lunatus*)	269 000
Kidney bean (*Phaseolus vulgaris*)	98 000-138 000
Common wheat (*Triticum vulgare*)	26 000

Apart from the theoretical interest of these different substances, their presence in foodstuffs, according to Gontzea, Ferrando and Sutzesco (1968), raises practical problems both for the methodology of research into the nutritive value of a diet or a particular food and also for the techniques employed in the cooking and industrial preparation of food products. A study published in France in 1971 by the *Institut national de la recherche agronomique* (INRA) stresses the effects of heat treatment on the quality of soybean proteins. Although the presence of inhibitors in a ration of food can reduce its protein efficiency and bring it below levels that, in the original state, seemed sufficient, the treatments applied to render these substances inactive can also destroy certain amino acids and vitamins. If one wants to be sure that products retain all their nutritive potential, then one must make sure that the temperature and the length of time employed in cooking or heating during industrial processing are sufficient, but do not exceed those required to eliminate the effect of the inhibitors or the phytohaemagglutinins, so as not to destroy any essential amino acids. As the criteria to establish the optimum temperature and duration of heat treatment are biological, the food processing industry should have biological methods available to check their technological processes.

Along with these two categories of natural antinutritive substances there are some other elements, especially among the leguminous plants, that cause flatulence. As Calloway has noted (1968, 1973), the formation of intestinal gas varies according to the individual. However, according to Berk (1968), flatulence is the main restriction on the consumption of leguminous beans, especially by young children. It would be useful, therefore, to have varieties that do not generate a lot of intestinal gas. The factors that cause it, according to Calloway (1973), seem to be the oligosaccharides (stachyose, raffinose, verbascose) as well as certain peptides acting together with enterobacteria, particularly *Clostridium perfringens*, that are normally present in the human digestive tract. Other microorganisms appear to act in the same way and leguminous plants may have, thanks to the previously mentioned compounds, a favourable action on the development of these enterobacteria. Rackiss *et al.* (1970) have shown that some isoflavones (syringic acid, ferulic acid and chlorogenic acid) seem to have an inhibitory action on the production of intestinal gas at doses of 15 to 30 mg. It is worth recalling that coffee contains some of these isoflavones (chlorogenic acid in particular), but it also contains an antithiamine (Somogyi, 1978).

Substances that chelate minerals in the diet

By chelating minerals in the diet, some organic compounds that are present in foodstuffs are liable to interfere with, or even prevent, their absorption in the intestines. This possibility has been known since the work of Mellanby (1920, 1922, 1924). Apart from certain organic acids, such as lactic acid and citric acid, the effects of which are minor, there are two acids that deserve more study: phytic acid and oxalic acid.

Phytic acid, which is present in the form of phytates in seeds, cereal by-products, oilseed cakes, cocoa, nuts, mandarins, oranges, lemons, etc., forms insoluble compounds with calcium, iron, magnesium, zinc, and also forms complexes with proteins. Phytic acid supplies unutilizable phosphorus and, moreover, immobilizes food minerals by chelating elements essential to the organism. Its ill effects were seen during the Second World War when, by force of circumstances, people were obliged to eat decalcifying wholemeal bread (to mention only the main mineral element chelated, which was calcium). Krebs and Mellanby (1943) showed the effects of brown and white bread on calcium balance. For a given intake of calcium, the balance becomes positive again in the third week following the removal of the phytate from the diet. Similar observations were made by Jacquot *et al.* (1944). Even in recent years, according to Zarel *et al.* (1972), the amount of phytic acid in flour produced in Iran varies from 88 to 759 mg/100 g and can cause illness in schoolchildren.

A large dose of phytic acid (1 percent) added to the diet of young animals (rats, piglets or chickens) reduces their growth.

In grain, phytic-bound phosphorus represents between 47 and some 90 percent of the total phosphorus.

According to Mellanby (1949) the calcium-depriving role of phytic-bound phosphorus, which can cause rickets or osteoporosis, is due to the formation of the mixed salts of calcium/sodium or calcium/magnesium (phytin).

However, grains also have varying amounts of a phytase. This enzyme, which can break down phytic acid, is plentiful in wheat, rye and barley. According to Hiller (1968), the breakdown of phytin is more marked in rye bread than in wheat bread. Only 6 percent of phytin remains in the former as opposed to 39 percent in the latter. Phytase thus seems more active in rye.

Much less phytase is found in oats and maize. Phytase is also destroyed by heat. Foods made from cassava, according to Joseph (1973), seem to be without any mineral-immobilizing effect, except for the peeled, washed and

TABLE 8. Average phytic-bound phosphorus content of selected foods

Food	Phytic phosphorus	
	mg/100 g	*% of total phosphorus*
Oats	208-355	50-88
Wheat	170-280 and over	47-86
Barley	70-300	32-80
Rye	247	73
Rice	157-240	68
Maize	146-353	52-97
Rye flour (95%)	160	56
Soybean	231-575	52-68
Walnut	120	24
Groundnut	205	57
Potato	14	35
Kidney bean	12	10
Carrot	0-4	0-16
Lemon	120	81
Orange	295	91
Mandarin	116	80
Date	23	28
Pistachio nut	176	75

Source: Gontzea, Ferrando and Sutzesco (1968).

cooked root, which is rich in phytic-bound phosphorus. Fermentation of the cassava reduces the amount of this phosphorus.

The mineral-immobilizing action of phytic acid, which is already considerable in itself, is further enhanced in cooking when the phytase is destroyed by heat. The use of chemicals in the bread-making process, in place of traditional yeasts, prevents phytases from breaking down phytic acid,. most of which remains intact, together with its harmful ability to chelate minerals.

TABLE 9. — Oxalic acid content of selected foods
(mg/100 g)

Food	Oxalic acid
Rhubarb	257-1 336
Sorrel	270-730
Spinach	320-1 260
Chard or spinach beet	300-920
Cultivated lettuce	5-20
Dandelion	5-25
Leek	23-89
Potato	20-141
Tomato	5-35
Eggplant	10-38
Various fruits (apple, pear, peach)	0-30 ($\bar{x}=15$)
Mandarin and orange	21-30
Blackcurrant	2-90
Fig	80-100
Cocoa	500-900
Coffee	50-150
Tea (leaves)	300-2 000 and even 2 280
Tea (infusion)	10.1-18.5

Source: Gotzea, Ferrando and Sutzesco (1968).

Hiller (1968) found that the longer the fermentation time of the dough the greater the phytase activity. This is a point in favour of the use of yeast, which is currently being replaced too often by chemicals[1].

The average phytic-bound phosphorus content of various foodstuffs is shown in Table 8.

Oxalic acid, which is another mineral-chelating agent, is a dibasic acid that is widely distributed among vegetables. It is found in large quantities in spinach, rhubarb, sorrel, beetroot, banana, tea, coffee and sesame seed. Oke (1969), in his review of this matter, notes that the level of oxalic acid in the food under consideration is reduced when the level of phosphorus increases.

Table 9 gives some figures on the level of oxalic acid in foods commonly eaten by man. They refer to determinations made on fresh produce.

Lennon and Tagle (1973) found 4.9 g of oxalic acid in the leaves, and 366.5 mg in the roots, of *Beta saccharata* (per 100 g of fresh produce). In the *rapacea* variety, which is eaten as a salad in Chile, these authors found 1.5 g of oxalate per 100 g of fresh produce. Oxalic acid forms soluble salts with sodium and potassium while the oxalates of calcium and magnesium are insoluble. The ill effects caused by the consumption of oxalic acid are of two kinds. First, it causes calcium deficiency both in man and in non-ruminant animals. Second, at higher doses of 1 to 2 g of body weight, it is toxic to the kidney in which oxalates can cause serious lesions. According to Singh, Kothari, and Sharma (1973), it can even affect the heart, as has been shown in experiments in dogs.

Attention should also be drawn to an anonymous note that appeared in *Nutrition Reviews* (1973b), to the effect that patients who had had a resection of the ileum showed considerable oxaluria, apparently caused by the high absorption of oxalates in the intestines. The diet of such subjects should be carefully controlled and it should contain as little oxalic acid as possible.

Based on the proportions in which oxalic acid and calcium react with each other, we can distinguish three categories of food:

● The first includes those foods where the oxalic-acid/calcium ratio is more than 3. This is the case of rhubarb, sorrel, spinach, cocoa and tea. It is necessary both to avoid an excessive intake of these foods and to supplement them with milk products capable of compensating for the calcium that is prevented from being assimilated by the excess of oxalic acid.

---

[1] The highest rates of pesticides are found in wholemeal bread since these are mainly located in the wheat husk and sifting removes them.

- The second includes foods where the oxalic-acid/calcium ratio is close to unity. This is the case with oranges, blackcurrants and potatoes, which present few drawbacks as regards oxalic acid contents.
- The third category includes foods where the oxalic-acid/calcium ratio is less than unity. These include haricot beans, celery, cabbages and endives, which are not included in the list given earlier as they are foods where the presence of oxalic acid can be ignored.

Finally, the effect of oxalic acid depends on the calcium of the diet that is still available for absorption after a portion of it has been chelated by the acid.

In a study of 10 children aged from 5 to 8 years it was noted that the consumption of spinach (or rather, the amount of oxalic acid supplied by such vegetables in the diet) causes no trouble when the diet is rich in milk and contains around 40 mg of calcium per kilogram of weight, i.e., in this case, between 0.8 to 1.3 g/day of calcium. One mg of calcium makes 2.25 mg of oxalic acid insoluble and neutralizes its action. Moreover, the boiling of vegetables and discarding the water in which the vegetables have been cooked [1] promote the elimination, in part, of the oxalic acid contained in the food. Unfortunately all vegetables are not always prepared in this way and, in this case, the diet should compensate for the presence of oxalic acid by an increase in calcium. This is all the more important as the normal diet of many people includes little calcium.

Excess of toxic minerals

This question has mostly been studied in the animal. Cases of illness are known in cattle grazing on land rich in selenium or molybdenum ('Teart' lands in southwest England). The general principle that emerges from such studies is that between a useful and a toxic dose of a trace mineral element for a given species there is a variable margin depending on the nature of the particular trace mineral element concerned. It is also worth stressing that pollution, particularly industrial pollution, can alter the basic nature of the problem. Excessive levels of trace mineral elements, originating in the soil and then found in food, may be harmful at varying doses depending on the particular trace mineral element involved. To these levels we must then add any excess due to pollution. Thus what was originally natural is now complicated by the artificial.

---

[1] Discarding the water is strongly recommended. It also eliminates any pesticides.

The advantages of the presence of molybdenum in maintaining low food levels of nitrosamines have already been mentioned. Excesses of this trace element in foodstuffs are not a concern in man, although they can be in ruminants.

Large doses of selenium can be toxic; wheat grown on soil rich in this element can contain from 10 to 30 $\mu g/g$ (Hogue, 1970). Animals suffer from chronic poisoning when the fodder, grain or seeds contain from 5 to 40 $\mu g/g$ of selenium. Selenium is more easily stored by undernourished animals. As regards comparative pathology, Hashem (1958) has considered the possibility of a relationship between cirrhosis of the liver among children in Egypt and an excess of selenium present in a poor diet. Selenium poisoning is more likely among people who are vegetarians (whether by choice or necessity) than among others who have a double plant-to-animal relay between the selenium in the soil and their own organism (i.e., soil-plant-animal-man, instead of just soil-plant-man).

Ku et al. (1973) have proved that the addition of 0.1 $\mu g/g$ of selenium to foods already containing between 0.24 and 0.45 $\mu g/g$ of this trace element does not increase its concentration in the long dorsal muscle nor in the kidneys of pigs; there is only a slight increase in the level of selenium in the liver. Nevertheless, according to Ku et al. (1972), there seems to be a linear correlation of 0.95 ($P < 0.01$) between the selenium in the diet and that found in the long dorsal muscle. However, as Cunha (1970) reports, there is no danger posed to the consumer of meat coming from animals whose diets contain 0.5 $\mu g/g$ of selenium. Generally, experts consider that this trace mineral element (the active prosthetic group of glutathione peroxidase) can be present without any danger, at the levels indicated above, in the diets of farm animals; and that at levels between 0.3 and 0.5 $\mu g/g$ in vegetables there is no risk to the consumer. Finally, according to Iwata, Okamoto and Ohsawa (1973), when doses of methylmercuric iodide are given per os over 8 to 10 days [1], doses of 0.5 mg/kg of body weight/day of sodium selenite prevent the loss of weight, specific symptoms and death. Scott (1973) discussed the problem well, in general terms.

The contamination of foodstuffs by mercury is a fact. Lu (1974) stated clearly that since mercury is widespread in the environment, it is found in all food products. The concentrations are, on average, very low (around 0.02 $\mu g/g$), although there can be considerable variations depending on the type of food and the level of contamination of the surroundings. The meat of

---

[1] See also an unsigned article (*Nutrition Reviews*, 1973a, 31:25) which states that the selenium found in tuna reduces the toxicity of the methylmercury that this fish sometimes contains. Since then this has been confirmed by several studies.

certain predatory fish, as well as that of fish caught in contaminated waters, can contain much more (0.5 to 5 μg/g). However, studies carried out by Evans and Jack (1972) on samples of fish caught in 1920 and 1965 and preserved in museums did not show much difference in mercury levels from those in samples caught in 1970. Quantitative analyses carried out by Tanner (1972) on various foods gave the following results:

Item	Mercury content ($\mu g/kg$)
Flour	< 50
Sugar, potatoes, beef	3
Chicken	3
Shrimps	14
Eggs	< 2
Whole milk	< 1
Powdered milk	10

Albano-Annichino, Intrieri and Zicarelli (1972) give the following levels for poultry products sold in the market of Naples: for 104 chickens examined ≤ 0.05 μg/g; for 105 eggs examined > 0.06 μg/g in three eggs only (0.06-0.07 and 0.10 μg/g).

There were no appreciable amounts of mercury in 93 percent of the chicken muscles and 76 percent of the eggs examined.

In the Federal Republic of Germany, according to Schelenz and Diehl (1973) the average intake of mercury from food and drink is 53 μg/week.

It should be noted that, in its sixteenth report (1973), the Joint FAO/WHO Expert Committee on Food Additives recommended a "temporary tolerable weekly intake" of 0.3 mg of total mercury per person, of which not more than 0.2 mg should be in the form of methylmercury (expressed as mercury). These figures correspond to 0.005 mg and 0.0033 mg per kg of body weight respectively. They were obtained by taking the lowest concentration of mercury in the hair (50 μg/g) observed at the beginning of intoxication at this concentration and applying the appropriate safety margin.

Lead is also taken in as a result of air pollution. According to Bazell (1971) automobile exhaust pipes spread 180 000 tons of lead over the entire United States. The levels of lead found in the bodies of zoo animals can reach 3 900 μg/g on a dry weight basis. A level of 6 μg/m^3 of air increases the excretion of coproporphyrins. In Denmark, according to Rebsdorf (1973), wild ducks have been poisoned by lead. It is fortunate that such ducks are not eaten every day [1].

In various preserved fruits and vegetables, Thomas, Roughan and Watters (1973) found, in 76 samples, an average of 0.56 μg/g of lead with a spread of 0.10 to 3.90 μg/g. In determining cadmium levels, these authors found an average of 0.02 μg/g with a spread of 0.01 to 0.18 μg/g. Sapetti, Ardvino and Durio (1973) noted that the administration of 1 to 5 g of lead to cows does not cause effects, but the milk produced is liable to contain up to 220 μg/l of heavy metal. Bovay (1970) noted that along the edges of roads there can be up to 100 mg of lead per kg of grass on a dry weight basis. The feeding of cows with such fodder naturally leads to an increase of lead in their milk. In his study, after only four weeks of such a diet the milk contained four times as much lead as that of the control animals. Cows grazing along the edges of highways can ingest as much as 1 300 mg of lead/day. The toxic dose, as Sapetti, Ardvino and Durio (1973) have shown, is much higher. Nevertheless, it is wise to take into consideration the phenomenon of accumulation. Moreover, the faeces of such cows increase the amount of lead in the soil, and this is another form of pollution.

The problem of the levels of cadmium in plants was studied by Schacklette (1972). The level is related to the amount in the soil. It differs from one region to another, as has been shown by the variations found during studies on moss in the southern states of the United States. The levels vary from 2.1 to 25.8 μg/g with the largest number of samples examined (20 out of 122) containing 8.5 μg/g.

To this cadmium in the soil should be added the amounts deriving from pollution, to which Tyler (1972) has drawn attention. As with lead, exhaust fumes are responsible. Industrial effluent and fumes also discharge cadmium into the ecosystem. Warren, Delavault and Fletcher (1971) indicate levels of between 1 and 2 μg/g in various vegetables, including lettuce, potatoes, cabbage, beetroot, haricot beans, all grown in country areas. However, in vegetables coming from industrial regions in Canada and the United Kingdom, levels of 87 μg/g have been found in lettuce, 12.7 μg/g in potatoes, 3.9 μg/g in cabbage, 2.4 μg/g in haricot beans and 3.0 μg/g in beetroot. Table 10 gives some figures derived from Schacklette (1972).

Cadmium is known to be toxic. Beginning with a level of 50 μg/g it lowers the growth rate of piglets and halts it completely when the level reaches 1 350 μg/g in the diet (Cousins, Barber and Trout, 1973). Cadmium seems to

---

[1] Ferrando and Milhaud found over 3 mg/kg on a fresh weight basis in 23 percent of the livers of dogs in the Paris region (unpublished, 1976).

TABLE 10. Levels of cadmium in selected plants
(*μg/g on dry weight basis*)

Plant or plant part	Concentration	
	Environment with normal levels of cadmium	Environment with levels of cadmium higher than normal
Grass	0.03-0.3	0.6-40
Maize grain	0.1	2
Polished rice	–	0.5
Grain of wheat, barley and oats	0.1-0.5	0.1-1.5
Asparagus	–	8
Lettuce	0.3-0.5	4-16 and over
Spinach	0.6-1.2	–
Tomato	–	2

prevent the development of the active metabolites of Vitamin D. According to an FAO/WHO publication (1972), an excess of cadmium (as with lead) can promote the occurrence of cardio-vascular disease in man. There seems to be a clear correlation between these diseases, their mortality rates and the levels of cadmium in milk, at least as regards the towns in the northern United States. Stoewsand (1972) attributes this to cadmium dust falling on pasture land. He estimates that man absorbs daily 70 μg of cadmium, 300 μg of lead, and 25 μg of mercury.

This rapid survey of the level of toxic mineral elements in foodstuffs shows, however, that it is rarely natural in origin. Usually the food that man eats, particularly plants and fish, does not contain these elements except as a result of industrial contamination of the environment [1]. In the long run, such pollution may change not only the characteristics of foods and their health-related properties but may also influence the agronomic conditions of their production. There is a shift in the development cycles of soil, plants and animals: the first two have greater tolerance to the effects of cumulation. This shift makes it impossible to foresee the outcome of ventures that a type of human "logic" is intent on following, but which nature could force man to abandon in the long, or not-so-long, term. For this reason, we should beware of altering the environment too much.

---

[1] A great many studies performed since 1975-1976 have confirmed this fact.

Antivitamins

The antivitamins, which are present in our food in the natural state, can interfere with the vitamins in the diet. They act in different ways. By an enzymatic process, they can even alter the molecule of the vitamin by splitting it into several inactive parts. They either hydrolyse vitamins or chelate them.

Finally, these antivitamins compete with the molecule and prevent it from acting in the metabolism, particularly when the vitamin and antivitamin are similar in structure. Mentzer (1947) defined these different modes of action when he stated that an antivitamin is any organic substance whose biological effects are identical to those caused by the lack of a given vitamin and whose action is reversible, i.e., it can be neutralized by the administration of this given vitamin. Meunier (1952) reviewed this matter, which had previously been examined as a whole in 1949 in the context of the feeding of domestic animals. The whole problem has also been studied by Lepkovsky (1966), Gontzea, Ferrando and Sutzesco (1968) and Somogyi (1973 and 1978).

In connection with the destruction of vitamins in the diet by enzymes, the thiaminases and ascorbic acid oxidase should be mentioned.

Substances capable of chelating and rendering a vitamin inactive include egg-white avidin and, perhaps, maize niacinogen.

As regards substances capable of acting by structural analogy, dicoumarol should be noted.

Foods and hormones that cause a particularly high intake of a particular vitamin should be excluded from this classification, nor should one consider as an antivitamin the antagonism that exists between one nutrient and another as a result of their linked metabolism, even though this has been done in the past. Such antagonism is a question of food balance rather than of a specific action, which is the case with an antivitamin. This concept has not always been fully understood and it is therefore worth stressing.

Thiaminases destroy vitamin B_1 or thiamine by splitting the molecule.

In this connection, the fundamental work carried out by Green and Evans (1940), Woolley (1941) and Woolley and Langsworth (1942) should be mentioned. Some foods are rich in this Vitamin-B_1-splitting enzyme, which is also found in the "thiaminolytic" intestinal bacteria that are also capable of rendering B_1 inactive.

A large number of fish, shellfish and other aquatic animals contain significant amounts of thiaminases. Of 31 species of fish caught in the Great Lakes area of the United States, 15 (including 4 varieties of carp) had thiaminolytic action, while of 9 marine species none could break down Vitamin B_1. However, this ability has been shown in herring, anchovy, etc.

TABLE 11. Resistance to heat of thiaminase found in the cephalothorax of crayfish (*Procambarus clarkii*)

Measure	Fresh	Boiled for 5 min	Boiled for 30 min	Dried in oven at 100°C for 24 h
Amount of thiamine destroyed (mg/min/g)	3.70 ± 0.32	1.02 ± 0.14	0.89 ± 0.07	0.52 ± 0.05
Specific activity (micromoles of thiamine destroyed/min/g)	0.0110	0.0030	0.0027	0.0015
Reduction of activity due to heat treatment (%)	–	72.3	75.8	85.9

Source: Rutledge and Levi (1972).

Ishihara, Yasuda and Morooka (1972) studied this enzyme in the anchovy; Ishihara, Kinari and Yasuda (1973) found thiaminase in the muscles and, naturally, the viscera of 7 species out of 11. In the Philippines, Luna Zenaida *et al.* (1968) observed this enzyme in 8 varieties of fish, 5 varieties of clam and 4 varieties of shellfish. Boiling and storage for three months increase thiaminase activity in these marine animals and salting the fish preserves the enzyme as well. Rutledge, Levi and Ying (1972) made similar observations on crayfish (*Procambarus clarkii*). In this shellfish, the thiaminase is located at the cephalothorax and remains active for up to 30 minutes in boiling water and for 24 hours in an oven at 100°C. All thiaminases are, therefore, not thermolabile as was previously thought. Table 11, taken from the work of the above-mentioned authors, illustrates this. This example shows that not even cooking can destroy certain types of thiaminases; an important dietary lesson should thus be drawn.

According to Kawasaki and Ono (1968) thiaminases are also found in mushrooms.

Ascorbic oxidase (ascorbase), identified by Tauber, Kleiner and Miskind (1935), changes ascorbic acid into dehydroascorbic acid and, if the reaction continues, into diketogulonic acid, oxalic acid, etc. When the plant is intact the enzyme is hardly active, but it is released from the cells in response to damage to the harvested plant. Optimum activity is found at around 38°C. The presence of this enzyme has been noted in cabbage, cucumbers, pumpkin, apples, lettuce, watercress, peaches, carrots, potatoes, tomatoes, bananas, etc. The activity of the enzyme varies greatly from one species, and from one variety, to another. It is mainly found in the outer parts of the fruit. Green fruit contains more than ripe fruit. Fruit should be eaten soon after it is picked and not kept too long because, even during the storage period, destruction is rapid and progressive and the product becomes rich in ascorbase.

The second type of antivitamin found in the natural state in foods acts by chelating the vitamins. The model for compounds acting in this way is egg-white avidin, which renders biotin inactive by forming an avidin-biotin complex. It was the discovery of biotin that made it possible to understand the harmful action of raw egg-white. Eakin, Snell and Williams (1940a, 1940b, 1941) gave an explanation of the mechanism involved. An avidin molecule combines with two molecules of biotin. The reaction is stoichio-metric. The compound formed is stable and not dialysable. Neither the digestive enzymes nor bacteria can dissociate this complex. Fortunately, cooking makes egg-white in general, and avidin in particular, lose this ability to chelate biotin. It should be noted that the avidin content in egg-white greatly surpasses that in egg-yolk. Trouble can develop when several raw eggs are eaten daily. One must always make sure that the white of the egg is fully coagulated. Three to five minutes' cooking in boiling water is usually sufficient for this.

Maize contains certain elements that hinder and can even prevent the utilization of niacin (Vitamin PP). An enzyme-resistant complex, niacino-gen, seems to be produced with this vitamin. Krehl, Strong and Elvehjem (1944) have checked this hypothesis indirectly by showing that mild alkaline treatment liberates the niacin, as shown by bacteriological assay of this vitamin. The existence of such alkaline action is, however, disputed and does appear doubtful. Gontzea, Ferrando and Sutzesco (1968) maintain that treating maize with alkalis has no effect. They believe that the antivi-tamin action of maize is much more complex, and that most of the research carried out in man, monkeys, pigs and dogs shows that dystrophy caused by maize is not simply owing to a deficiency but has a complex pathogenesid that cannot be explained solely in connection with Vitamin PP. In support of this view, and to illustrate the difficulties that arise in studying the matter, the work of Mérimée and Eineberg (1973) should be mentioned. Accord-ing to them, ordinary maize or 'Opaque-2' (which is rich in lysine) seems to lower the secretion of the growth hormone in man after 22 to 24 days of a diet based on maize.

The third group of substances having an antivitamin action includes the compounds that compete directly with the molecule of the vitamin in question. The inhibition is molecular, sometimes as a result of a structural

**TABLE 12. Main antivitamins found in food
that act by structural analogy**

Food or drink	Compound	Vitamin neutral- ized	Reference
Fodder, particularly sweet clover	Dicoumarol	K	Stahmann, Huebner and Link, 1941
Haricot bean (*Phaseolus vulgaris*)	Unknown	E	Bandyopadhyay, 1970
Alfalfa	Unknown	E	Singsen *et al.*, 1955
Bracken (*Pteris aquilina*)	3,4-dihydroxycinnamic acid	B_1	Somogyi, 1971
Bilberry	Four factors including 3,4-dihydroxycinnamic acid	B_1	Hilker, 1968
Coffee	As for bilberry + chloro- genic acid and pyro- catechins	B_1	Boenicke and Czok, 1970
Cereals	Not known but potential- ity analogous to 4-deoxy- piridoxine	B_6	Mickelsen, 1968; Mickelsen and Yang, 1966; Tjostem, 1965
Linseed meal	Linatine which yields *l*-a- mino-*D*-proline	B_6	Kratzer and Williams, 1948; Klosterman, 1974
Gyromitra (*Gyromitra esculenta*)	Gyromitrine, N-methyl- N-formylhydrazine and methylhydrazine	B_6	Klosterman, 1974
Agaritine (*Agaricus bisporis*)	Agaritine, γ-glutamyl, a derivative of 4-hydroxy- methyl phenylhydrazine	[1] B_6	

[1] Only one clinical case has been recorded in man of illness following the ingestion of antivitamin B_6 (Klosterman, 1974).

similarity between the two. These chemical compounds, which are closely similar to each other and which in some way "deceive" the metabolic systems are, according to Mentzer (1947) and Meunier (1952), true antivitamins.

Table 12 lists the activities of the main antivitamins belonging to this third category that can be found in the natural foods of man and animals. Many of these antivitamins are compounds that counteract the activity of vitamins in the B complex. Daniel (1961) examined this question in detail, although he was mainly concerned with synthetic compounds not found in foodstuffs.

Molasses could have been added to the list in Table 12 as it can cause necrosis of the cerebral cortex in ruminants. However, as this effect is limited to these animals, it would be wrong to link effects noted in ruminants to a mechanism depending on the antivitamin effect of molasses. This mechanism is more complex and is related to the question of dietary balance. The fact that symptoms and lesions disappear upon administration of a vitamin does not necessarily imply that the symptoms and lesions were due to an antivitamin. This would be too simple. Besides, there is no necrosis of the cerebral cortex in rats deprived of thiamine. As stated earlier, dietary imbalance can very easily involve an increased use of a particular vitamin. Large amounts of molasses can ferment into alcohol in the rumen. The antivitamin theory is not a universal panacea. All the same, several common foods can add a genuine antivitamin action to such dietary imbalance. This should be remembered when drawing practical conclusions that affect current feeding habits.

Hormones and antihormones

Dohrn, Faure and Blorevogel (1926), Fellner (1926) and Loewe, Lange and Spohr (1927) were the first to indicate the existence of oestrogenic substances in plants[1]. Since then numerous studies on plant extracts have shown the presence of this effect. Female mammals and birds are thus not the only sources of hormones capable of having an oestrogenic effect.

Shoeller isolated a compound from *Butea superba* that showed strong oestrogenic activity. In 1946, Bennetts, Underwood and Shier discovered a similar compound in subterranean clover (*Trifolium subterraneum*). This compound, the methyl ester of genistein, was responsible for a series of miscarriages noted among ewes in Australia. Since then many studies have shown the abundance in nature of compounds having hormonal properties.

Compounds having antihormonal properties have also been found. In particular, it has already been noted that plants of the mustard family (but also those belonging to other families) show antithyroid effects. There is no doubt, therefore, that foodstuffs contain substances with hormonal effects capable of influencing the consumers' health, either directly, or relayed indirectly by animals. Nevertheless, as Perrault, Boisselot-Lefebvre and

---

[1] For a historical account of this subject see Ferrando and Ratsimamanga (1960).

Ratsimamanga remarked in 1960, given the considerable role played by hormones in the metabolism, this influence can be both harmful (when the exogenous intake is excessive) or beneficial if it is moderate; but this depends on the hormone or antihormone involved. They went on to stress how it is often surprising in developing countries, and even in Europe, that, in spite of a diet that is unbalanced and deficient in energy, protein and vitamins, the physical aspect of the consumer continues to be satisfactory. There is a widespread tendency to look only at the negative aspect of these questions; here, however, the positive aspects will be considered first.

Ratsimamanga, Mondain-Monval-Gérondeau and Diot in 1962 showed that when a rat under the age of puberty was fed a synthetic diet, that is, one lacking in hormones, for about 10 days, its development was retarded compared with a control group receiving hormones in their diet. Not only is there a slowing down of body development, but the ovaries, the thymus and the uterus are not normal. The addition of vitamins does not re-establish the physiological equilibrium. To achieve this, both vitamins and hormones are required.

Research carried out by Ferrando, Ratsimamanga and Boisselot-Lefebvre (1960a and b) showed that milk given to young rats at weaning has a marked effect on their growth in general. This is accompanied by changes in the weight of certain organs, particularly the internal secretory glands. Milk extract, containing only the sex hormones and the active corticoids, produced analogous effects on the rat deprived of adrenal glands. The results observed, particularly the weight decrease of the pituitary gland and the testicles in the male, and the increase in weight of the ovaries of the female, would seem to indicate a predominantly oestrogenic hormonal effect inhibiting the male functions. The same authors also observed an effect on the thyroid. Vague and Garrigues (1957) had previously drawn attention to the presence of oestrogens in several foods of animal origin.

Since then, other studies have confirmed the fact that milk contains hormones. In particular, Vogt and de Karg (1971) carried out studies not only on milk but on other foods of animal origin, such as eggs and meat. Pellerin and Bourgain (1973) also found oestrogens, progesterone and corticosteroids in milk, which, in addition, contains numerous enzymes and which increases movement in the ileum in guinea-pigs and the jejunum in rabbits in the same way as acetylcholine does (El-Karimi and Hilmy Mehdi, 1971).

In meat, liver, brain, milk and human colostrum there are considerable quantities of adrenal hormones (0.5 to 1.10 mg per 100 g expressed in deoxycorticosterone [DOC]). Meat, on an equal weight basis, represents an adrenal activity equivalent to 10 percent of that of the gland itself. The consumption of around 100 g of brain provides 1.14 mg of 17-hydroxycorticosteroids. According to Perrault, Boisselot-Lefebvre and Ratsimamanga (1960), the level in the brain represents a third of the value found in the adrenal gland of the same animal, per unit weight. Finally, 100 g of liver provide 13 mg of a compound whose properties resemble those of deoxy-corticosterone.

Thus, much research work, even though it has not been carried out systematically, has shown that most foods of animal origin contain hormónes that generally can be extracted and identified. Sharaf and Gomara (1971) have noted that vitamins E, C and B_6 possess the synergistic oestrogen properties of oestradiol in increasing the weight of the uterus of ovariectomized rats.

As has been mentioned, plants can also have hormonal and antihormonal effects. These are known either because they interfere with the reproduction of animals, or because of their traditional uses — an example of this is the use made of *Stevia rebaudiana* B. by Indians of the Mato Grosso as a

TABLE 13. Level of diethylstilboestrol (DES) equivalent found in wheat grown on land treated with various fertilizers, 1961, 1962

($\mu g/100$ g on a dry weight basis)

Fertilizer	Level of DES equivalent	
	1961	1962
Control group without fertilizer	0.20	0.45
With N + P + K mixture	0.32-0.64	1.76
With farm manure	0.65-0.92	3.90

Source: Ferrando, Guilleux and Guérillot-Vinet (1961).

contraceptive concoction (Planas and Kuć, 1968). The flowers and stems are active and can reduce fertility in the rat even 50 to 60 days after its administration.

The substances extracted from plants that have a hormonal effect on the genitals or other endocrine glands are not steroids, with a few exceptions, but are generally flavones, isoflavones, coumarins, triterpenoids, etc.

Functional analogues, linked to triterpenes, have been isolated from plants. For example, liquorice contains glycyrrhizic acid, which has a hormonal effect on adrenalectomized rats. *Centella asiatica* (from Madagascar) produces asiatic and arjunolic acids with identical properties. Too much liquorice, or drinks based on it, can be harmful and has, in fact, caused adverse effects on consumers. In principle, one should always be aware of the need to vary one's food and drink.

Generally speaking, the levels of hormonal substances in plants vary according to conditions of cultivation. In 1952, Alexander and Rossiter observed that clover grown on land poor in phosphorus was usually richer in oestrogenic substances. It has been shown that a similar phenomenon is found with wheat and carrots, in a reverse direction: the level of oestrogenic substances in these two plants is highest when they are grown on fields fertilized with farm manure (see Tables 13 and 14).

The 1962 results, which are shown in these tables together with those published in 1961, show the action of the fertilizers as well as the difference due to the year of the harvest. It is evident, thus, that the factors affecting the levels of compounds that have hormonal activity in food are many and varied.

TABLE 14. Level of diethylstilboestrol (DES) equivalent found in carrots grown on land treated with various fertilizers, 1961, 1962

(µg/100 g)

Fertilizer	Level of DES equivalent			
	1961		1962	
	Fresh produce	Dry produce	Fresh produce	Dry produce
Control group without fertilizer	0.12-0.16	0.6-0.8	0.5	3.3
With N + P + K mixture	0.24-0.26	1.2-1.3	0.7	3.4
With farm manure	0.40	2.0	0.8	4.0

Source: Ferrando, Guilleux and Guérillot-Vinet (1961).

Tables 15, 16 and 17 give some qualitative and quantitative values related to substances with hormonal activity. Table 15 refers to products of animal origin, although the levels in grass and alfalfa are also indicated. These levels can on occasion be higher than stated. Standara and Chury (1973) found coumestrol in the sperm of rabbits feeding on alfalfa. The degeneration of the egg and the fecundatory disorders seen in females after they have been covered could be due to the presence of this hormone.

**TABLE 15. Qualitative and quantitative values
of hormones found in various foods**

Food	Oestrogenic hormones (mg/100 g)	Androgenic hormones	Adrenal hormones (mg/100 g)
Milk	0.002 to 0.01 Wide variations depending on physiological circumstances	1 to 100 IU per litre	0.005 to 0.20
Meat	0.04 to 0.13 (in dimethylhexoestrol) Chicken muscles treated with oestrogens for seven days Present in non-treated chickens	Present	0.01 to 0.10 (in corticosteroids)
Brain	–	–	up to 1.14 (in deoxycorticosterone)
Animal fats	0.3 to 2.2 (in oestrone)	–	–
Vegetable fats	0,52 (in oestrone)	–	–
Grass, alfalfa	0.001 to 0.01 (in oestrone) 0.002 to 0.006 (in diethylstilboestrol)	–	–

Bickoff (1968) found compounds with oestrogenic action in coffee, wheat, barley, oats, potatoes, rhubarb, haricot beans, apples and garlic. The compounds he found are as follows: oestrone, α-oestradiol, equilenin, equilin, coumestrol, genistein, daidzein, biochania A, formononetin. The consumption of onions has a favourable effect on the weight of the testicles (Sharaf, 1967). According to the same author, onion juice has hypoglycaemic properties and acts *in vitro* on the contraction of the uterus. Attrep, Mariani and Attrep (1973) have also found in the yellow onion a compound analogous to prostaglandin A_1.

TABLE 16. Oestrogens in various animal fats
(mg/100 g of fat)

Food	Kober folliculin	Allen-Doisy (in oestrone equivalent)
Cow fat	37	1.0
Pig fat	21	0.3
Horse fat	–	2.3
Lard	3.5	0.4
Mutton fat	4	0.1
Butter	28	0.8
Colostrum (human)	–	0.1
Whale-liver oil	–	3.2

Source: Vague and Garrigues (1957). See also *Anabolic agents in animal production. FAO/WHO Symposium, Rome, March 1975,* ed by F.C. Lu and J. Rendel. Stuttgart, Tieme.

TABLE 17. Level of oestrogen in selected vegetable oils and fats
(mg/100 g of fat)

Vegetable oils and fats	Kober folliculin	Allen-Doisy (in oestrone equivalent)
Olive (pressed)	15	4.00
Olive (extract of cake)	35	5.20
Refined olive	5	0.25
Groundnut	10	0.25
Linseed	3.5	0.20
Soybean	10	0.80
Rapeseed	8	1.00
Palm	14	0.90
Copra	5	0.20
Shea tree	11	0.70
Sesame	0	0
Commercial maize	11	1.50
Sunflower seed	18	0.50
Cocoa butter	3	0.80

Source: Garrigues (1957).

For a long time hops, and beer, were considered to be highly oestrogenic. A study by Fenselau and Talalay (1973) carried out on hops grown on various soils in Europe and in the United States, either directly or after saponification, indicates that this plant is not oestrogenic in mice under the age of puberty.

In concluding this review of the hormonal effects of foodstuffs, mention should be made of the oestrogenic activity of the zearalenone isolated from moulds of the *Fusarium* genus, which contaminates maize (Jemmali, 1973). Jemmali's findings have been confirmed by numerous other studies.

Antigonadotropic substances are found in rice germ (Kobori, Yoshimura and Nakane, 1957) and, according to Mérimée and Eineberg (1973), maize lowers the secretion of the growth hormone in man. It is, in fact, almost exclusively in foods of vegetable origin that there is evidence of antihormonal substances or, to be more precise, of substances acting on the thyroid gland. Although these compounds are also present in foods of animal origin, milk in particular, this is because the animals had eaten the plants as part of their diet. Their physiological effect is always to inhibit, to a varying degree, the function of the thyroid. The identity of compounds that have this antithyroid action is now known. They include thiocyanates and iso-thiocyanates derived either from sulphur-containing heterosides or from the sulphur-conjugated cyano-compounds, cheirolin produced by the hydrolysis of glucocheirolin, iberin and, finally, progoitrin or glucorapipherin (another thioglucoside obtained from various Cruciferae), which hydrolyses under the action of mirosinase to give goitrin or 5-vinyl-2-thiooxazolidone.

Although cooking inactivates an enzyme, hydrolysis can still take place in the organism. Other compounds of the polyphenol family also have antithyroid action. They are found in groundnuts and in the cashew nut (*Anacardium occidentale*), which is eaten in India. The compounds come from the hydrolysis of two glycosides, arachidoside and anacardioside. Propyl-disulphide found in onions and garlic may also have antithyroid action (Cowan, Saghir and Salji, 1967; Saghir, Cowan and Salji, 1967). Moreover, an oligopeptide consisting of two or three amino acids with antithyroid activity has been isolated from soybeans by Konijn, Gershon and Guggenheim (1973).

It was noted in 1932 that marrow cabbage disturbs gestation in the sheep. The number of live and normal lambs born was half that of the control groups. The thyroid of the stillborn lambs was 11 times heavier than that of healthy animals. Similar observations were made by Peltola (1960) in Finland. The substances responsible were found to be thiocyanates (Wright, 1958; Clements, 1960; Clements and Wishart, 1956).

The milk of cows fed on marrow cabbage can contain up to 5.6 mg per 100 ml of thiocyanates while that of animals grazed on pasture land shows only

0.8 mg per 100 ml. Serious effects were seen not only in calves, but also in children given such milk. The thyroid gland in calves born to cows who were themselves affected showed a reduction in colloid substances and an increase in follicular cells, etc. The level of thiocyanates shows seasonal variation. It is high in summer, when it can reach 15 mg per litre, and falls to 2 mg per litre in winter. More recent figures given by Hoppe, Kozlowska and Rutkowski (1971) relating to the milk of cows fed colza cake show that cows receiving 1.8 kg per day of a concentrate containing 38 percent of this cake together with 5.8 to 6.2 mg of 5-vinyl-2-thiooxazolidone, 0.8 to 0.9 mg of isothiocyanates and 0.2 mg of thiocyanates produce milk containing 5.71 mg of thiocyanates per litre. The milk from the morning milking has the most thiocyanates. According to Rutkowski, Kozlowska and Hoppe (1972) about 25 percent of the thioglucosides in the diet are transferred to the milk. Iwarsson *et al.* (1973) have shown that 15 percent of rapeseed in a concentrate fed to bull-calves 6 to 12 months old caused alterations in their thyroids. The same authors found that, when rats were fed milk from cows that had a concentrate in their diet of 20 to 25 percent rapeseed cake, the thyroids of the rats were affected. The level of iodine in the milk was also lowered.

Table 18 shows the main foodstuffs liable to have a direct antithyroid effect on the consumer or an indirect one passed on by cows, sheep or milch goats. Only those foods whose effects on man have been proved are mentioned here. Wolff and Varrone (1969) believe that the methylxanthines may also have antithyroid activity. This activity increases in strength in the following scale:

Theophylline   >   Caffeine   >   Theobromine
(Tea)   (Coffee)   (Chocolate)

This effect also seems to exist in the walnut (*Juglans regia*). It acts indirectly by accelerating faecal excretion of thyroxine (Linazasoro, Sanchez Martin and Jimenez-Diaz, 1970). Walnuts could therefore be used by those suffering from hyperthyroidism.

It is possible to reduce the levels of sulphur-containing antithyroid compounds in plants. Sedlak, Langer and Michajlovski (1966) believe that this can be achieved by not using fertilizers that are rich in sulphur and by reducing the use of nitrates during the period of cultivation. It is also advisable not to give cows feedstuffs liable to enrich their milk with antithyroid compounds in regions where there is a lack of iodine and when the milk is destined for children or invalids.

TABLE 18. Foods with direct or indirect antithyroid activity

Foods	Activity	
	Direct	Indirect via milk
Anacardium occidentale: cashew nut	+	−
Arachis hypogaea: groundnut	+	+ (?)
Brassica napus: rape	−	+
Brassica napus var. *oleifera:* rapeseed and rapeseed cake	−	+
Brassica oleracea var. *botrytis* subvar. *cymosa:* broccoli	+	−
Brassica oleracea var. *capitata:* common cabbage, red and white	+	−
Brassica oleracea var. *gongyloides:* kohlrabi	+	−
Brassica oleracea var. *medullosa:* marrow cabbage	−	+
Daucus carota: carrot	+	−
Soja hispida: soybean	+	+ (?)
Trifolium repens var. *album:* white clover	−	+

Note: + = activity exists; − = no activity.

Finally, the role that phytohormones could have on man should be noted. According to Vlitos (1960), the nature of such a role is highly speculative. Studies have been carried out with indoleacetic acid and gibberellins, but they have not arrived at conclusive results.

The facts set out above show how important this question of hormones and antihormones in food is. It is related to agriculture and animal husbandry and, ultimately, to human pathology and physiology as well.

It is important that basic research be carried out and a systematic study made on what happens to the hormones in food between harvest and consumption. One should also study their metabolism in the organism and isolate their physiological effects in relation to the organism's endogenous hormone production; in other words, a precise balance between the two should be drawn up.

Moreover, as regards human nutrition, if we take the case of milk, which is the perfect, complete food, it contains, apart from its major components, various other substances that have hormonal properties: oestrogens, androgens, corticosteroids, antithyroids and, perhaps, even stimulins. Enough details have already been given of the repercussions the ingestion of milk can have on various internal secretory glands.

It would be interesting to see if substances of vegetable origin, particularly those with an oestrogenic action that are eaten by animals, act directly or after metabolic changes, and if the products of such transformations can accumulate in fat, meat and milk and, in turn, exert a physiological effect on the human consumer.

This question of oestrogenic substances is important, since they are so widespread in nature. In one type of clover, the presence of these substances is enough to disturb gestation in sheep and it is their presence in milk that seems to retard the sexual development of the male rat and hastens that of the female. In alfalfa, they promote the fattening of cattle and disturb the reproduction of rabbits.

It is necessary to note, however, that a good number of compounds with oestrogenic action on animals are eliminated after glucuronic conjugation and that humans only consume, in the end, the hormones of the animal involved, which are not absorbed by the digestive tract. In any case, when they are absorbed, they are rapidly excreted after glucuronic conjugation. It is not advisable, however, to administer through food hormones that are likely to disturb the endocrinal balance of certain sick persons. Boyland (1967) pointed out that a stilbestrol residue equivalent to 10 μg of oestradiol could activate endocrine tumours or pose a risk of tumours in women going through menopause. It is true, of course, that this is a synthetic non-steroid hormone that is absorbed by the intestine.

In any case, a thorough scientific study of such problems, which until now have been resolved too empirically, is certain to produce some surprises. Its absence complicates the question of balanced food supplies; a full analytical examination of the diet is as yet lacking and should be pursued systematically.

Carcinogenic agents in plants

Direct carcinogenic action by human foods is exceptionally rare. Generally speaking, a food can acquire such properties through contamination, by moulds for example, or else through modifications caused by processing. This subject will be dealt with in the second section of this book.

There are carcinogenic properties among plants of the genera *Senecio*, *Crotalaria* and *Heliotropium*, due to the presence of pyrrolizidine alkaloids, but this is of no importance except with animals. Experiments with calves and mice show that the milk of cows fed *Senecio* is not carcinogenic.

Safrole (*p*-allylmethylenedioxybenzene) is a condiment used in cooking and the preparation of drinks and seems to be carcinogenic when used in the diet over a long period at levels above 0.5 percent. The action of pepper and other spices was noted when we looked at the problem of nitrosamines. According to Ambrose, Cox and De Eds (1958), sesamol also has some properties that cause concern.

Cycad nuts contain glycosides one of which, cycasine, can be hydrolysed by an enzyme in the plant or by the enzymes of intestinal bacteria. The hydrolysis causes the formation of methylazoxymethanol which has hepatocarcinogenic properties similar to those of dimethylnitrosamine. In certain countries these nuts are used as food or as medicine (Laqueur *et al.*, 1963).

From a general point of view it should be noted that Weisburger (1971) found that cycasine does not cause cancer in "axenic" rats. The role of intestinal flora in the hydrolysis of the glycoside in cycad nuts has been well demonstrated. These inter-relationships between intestinal flora and the composition of the diet should be stressed. The consumption of foods rich in cellulose is thought to prevent the intestinal mucosa (particularly that of the large intestine) from being exposed to products resulting from the breakdown of fats, sterols and biliary acids by the intestinal flora, by accelerating the movement of food through the intestines. Some of these products, especially those similar to 20-methylcholanthrene, could be carcinogenic (Hill *et al.*, 1971). There would appear to be differences, however, between the activity of intestinal flora. Reddy, Baudura and Wynder (1973) and Reddy, Weisburger and Wynder (1974) showed that the intestinal flora of Americans in the western United States are more able to hydrolyse glucuronic-acid conjugates than the intestinal flora of Japanese, Chinese, vegetarians and members of the Seventh Day Adventist sect. These Americans daily excrete more coprostanols, coprostanones and neutral sterols than the others. There appears to be a close relationship between incidences of cancer of the colon and the excretion of these biliary acids and neutral sterols. The faeces of people who eat large amounts of meat have a β-glucuronidase activity of 20 ± 2.5 as against 5.6 ± 0.98 per mg of dry matter in people who do not eat meat.

Bracken is also thought to contain carcinogenic agents that cause cancer of the intestines in cows. These agents pass into the milk and can, in turn, cause cancer in humans (WHO, 1974). As mentioned earlier, the contrary is true in the case of *Senecio*.

Various actions

What may be called the "pharmacodynamics" of foodstuffs is an extremely vast subject. Throughout this study it has appeared in attempting to classify the properties of foods according to their particular effect on the consumer. There are also other influences, less specific but equally important, to be aware of. These will be considered here, in closing.

Certain fruits and vegetables can contain cholinesterase inhibitors. Orgell (1963) studied the effects of the extracts of 256 plants on human cholinesterase, including the extract of potato tubers, which proved to be the most active inhibitor. The information that follows has been taken from Grosby's review (1966) of the whole subject. Apart from in potatoes, cholinesterase inhibitors are also found in pepper, certain types of cabbage, pimentos, carrots, tomatoes, apples and oranges. The distribution of these inhibitors, which are also found in alfalfa and white clover (*Trifolium repens*), varies according to the part of the plant considered. According to Grosby, these substances account for some cases of illness that have been observed in children and animals. One can imagine that among these inhibitors it should be possible to find compounds with chemical structures that are non-toxic to mammals and that could be synthesized and used as new types of insecticides. Apart from this attractive possibility, these facts should also be related to the conclusions that can be drawn regarding human health and to the dangers it is exposed to through the use of pesticides in modern farming. Nature has preceded man in his fight against insects and parasites. These natural residues, however, have never caused concern to the experts. Who knows what would emerge if they were to be studied systematically and with the same methodologies as are used for the synthetic product? Remember that saponins in various vegetable fodders (Applebaum, Shlomo and Birk, 1969), L-dopa in seeds of the *Mucuna* genus (Rehr, Jansen and Feeny, 1973), gossypol in cotton seed and, finally, the antitrypsins mentioned earlier — that all these are part of the plant's defence against insects.

An article in *Chemical and Engineering News* (1974a) reported that research workers had discovered that concanavalin, a vegetable protein in haricot beans, can cause a syndrome in laboratory animals that is identical to that of rheumatism in man.

Abortifacient, teratogenic and numerous mutagenic compounds, including caffeine, are also found in plants. Those usually cited as having abortifacient properties are, fortunately, not edible except for the genera *Brassica* and *Lathyrus*.

But it is mainly in livestock, according to Keeler (1972), that plants are responsible for cases of teratogenesis. Keeler gives a list of deformations occurring in sheep and of the compounds capable of producing them. Nevertheless, one should bear in mind that toxic effects can be passed on to man through the consumption of meat or milk of animals that have fed on poisonous plants. This was what happened to a group of people who ate quail (found to be poisonous by Sergent [1941]) that had fed on the fruit of hemlock (*Conium maculatum*) without themselves suffering any untoward effects. There are other compounds with similar properties that are found in foods consumed by humans. Caffeine given to mice at doses of between 0.2 and 0.5 mg/g by subcutaneous injection at the 7th-8th day of gestation causes foetal reabsorption and, when the injection is given at the 9th-14th day this causes abnormalities in the limbs (Snigorska and Bartel, 1970). A drop in foetal weight was also observed by Gilbert and Pistey (1973) when doses of between 4 and 16 mg/day of caffeine were given by intraperitoneal injection, and they also noted a suppression of embryonic development at doses close to those absorbed by heavy coffee drinkers. But this is not the view of Thayer and Kensler (1973), who used doses of caffeine equivalent to those of a man drinking between 19 and 30 cups of coffee a day! Caffeine has also been accused of being a mutagen. Weinstein, Mauer and Solomon Hervey (1972) claim the opposite and the question is still unresolved.

The fact that caffeine increases lipolysis and modifies glucose tolerance could be the reason why there are so many diabetics in industrial areas, where, generally speaking, the people drink a lot of coffee. According to Haslbeck and Mehnert (1971), a study carried out in Munich showed that from 3 to 4 percent of the population were diabetics. Nevertheless, the authors think that one should be wary of drawing conclusions on this subject. Finally, Kowalewski (1973) showed that caffeine stimulates gastric secretion. Increase in the production of gastric juice is not accompanied by any change in composition.

There are numerous publications on the drawbacks of various foodstuffs. The hourly administration to rats of a 7-to-8-percent glucose solution suppresses food intake, causes weight loss and leads to death. A 3.5-percent solution does not have these effects (Sclafavi, 1973). Energy depletion does not seem to be the sole cause of this action; it may also be due to a hypersecretion of insulin. The harmful effects of certain oils, such as rapeseed[1],

---

[1] See FAO. *Dietary fats and oils in human nutrition. Report of an Expert Consultation,* 46 pages and annexes. Rome, 1977. FAO Food and Nutrition Paper No. 3.

are well known. The matter will not be discussed here but the reader is referred to the studies done by Rocquelin *et al.* (1973a, b) and to those of Kramer *et al.* (1973), which also raise doubts about maize oil (albeit when heated to around 200°C for 24 hours).

However, some favourable actions should also be noted. Garlic is quite definitely bactericidal as regards *Staphylococcus aureus* and *citreus, Escherichia coli, Pseudomonas* and *Klebsiella* (Sharaf *et al.*, 1969). According to Neeman, Lifshitz and Kashman (1970), avocado pears contain eight compounds with antibacterial action. The most active, 1,2,4-trihydroxyheptadeca-16-ene, seems to inhibit certain gram-positive bacteria at levels of 4 µg/ml. The bactericidal properties of pepper are also known. Rivers and Hill (1971) have shown that chow, an Ethiopian condiment that is 70 percent *Capsicum frutescens* and is used at levels of between 5 and 11 percent in food, inhibits the development of *Staphylococcus aureus, Salmonella typhimurium* and *E. coli.* It prevents food poisoning.

One of the components of pepper, capsidiol, is an antifungal sesquiterpene induced in the fruit by various moulds which transform it into a ketone derivative, the less toxic capsenone (Stoessl, Unwin and Ward, 1973). This capsidiol-capsenone interaction inhibits germination of spores but not mycelial growth. In this field, Masquelier published a study in 1968 on natural antibiotics in foodstuffs. He states, rightly, that the existence of these substances is perfectly normal and that the absence of natural antibiotics would be surprising. He says that more than 20 percent of the plants that have been examined so far contain substances that, *in vitro,* inhibit various bacterial cultures. He lists them in a table which is reproduced on the next page (Table 19).

The betel nut, *Areca catechu,* which is chewed by many people in India, is also cited. Its alcoholic extract acts at 1/10 000 on numerous bacteria and moulds.

Wine has already been mentioned; its bactericidal action on *Salmonella typhi* is due to anthyocyanins. Mention should also be made of phenolic acids in the cinnamic group (paracoumaric, ferulic, caffeic, gallic, chlorogenic acids, etc.). Tea also seems to have an antiviral activity.

The rather low activity of these antibiotics is compensated for by their abundance. The actual effect, therefore, is not negligible.

Masquelier (1968) has also drawn attention to the anti-tumour properties of certain plants such as *Rumex hymensoepalus* (tanner's dock), a close relative of sorrel. The active component, leucocyanidol, is a leucoanthocyanin.

In this connection, it should be noted that the analysis of foodstuffs can be disturbed by these natural compounds during the investigation of antibiotics that have been experimentally added.

TABLE 19. Antibiotic activities of selected foods

Origin	Active principle	Maximum activity *in vitro*	
Allium cepa (onion)	not identified	0.7 per 100 000	*B. abortus*
Allium sativum (garlic)	allicin	0.8 per 100 000	*Salmonella Shigella, Vibrio, Streptococcus*
Humulus lupulus (hop)	humulon lupulon	1 per 100 000	*C. diphteriae M. tuberculosis Streptococcus Staphylococcus*
Pyrus malus (apple)	phloretol	3 per 100 000	*Staphylococcus*
Numerous vegetables	quercitol	1 per 10 000	*B. abortus Salmonella E. coli Staphylococcus*
Lycopersicon esculentum (tomato)	tomatine	1 per 5 000	*C. albicans* Tinea fungi
Egg-white	lysozyme	0.1 per 100 000	*M. lysodeikticus*

Source: Masquelier (1966).

Finally, a protective role is played by essential oils produced by certain plants (Slavenas, 1967). These fragrant secretions are sometimes employed in cooking without our knowing their harmful or beneficial effects, apart, that is, from their gastronomic reputation.

There seems to be a general phenomenon of competition built into biological equilibria. This competition controls (as Darwin noted) not only the creation of species but also their preservation. There are, as we have seen, toxic moulds; but there are other very well known ones that are beneficial, either directly or indirectly. For this reason they have revolutionized animal husbandry and therapeutics. Mainguy (1949) has rightly drawn attention to these facts.

It will be seen later that to these natural advantages and disadvantages should be added the results of changes occurring during the production, storage or cooking of foods through the formation of new compounds that are harmful to the consumer. Even though cooking can inhibit certain antinutritive substances (e.g., antitrypsins), the cooking process can have other drawbacks. It can thus be stated that nothing is absolute in this field. The same process can sometimes be advantageous and sometimes harmful.

Are we really then surrounded by natural poisons to which are added those caused by pollution?

The pessimists would answer yes. The optimists would deny it and produce just as many proofs to support their views. The toxicologist knows, however, of the existence of these substances which experiments have shown to be more or less harmful. He also knows that the human body possesses efficient defence mechanisms and a great ability to adapt to circumstances, which enable it to counteract substances that are of moderate or medium toxicity or added doses of them that are of similar magnitude. It would be useful, therefore, to warn consumers against the myth of the "natural". "Pollution" can be found in the natural state as well. It can be found in the corners of the most out-of-the-way vegetable plot in the world, in fresh meadow grass and in the tastiest fruits; in the fireplace where our grandparents smoked their hams and in the pots and pans of our kitchens. To put it simply, everything that is natural is not necessarily perfect. What is natural may be good, even excellent, but it can also be less good and, sometimes, the worst thing possible. So, once again, it would be wise not to go to extremes. In biology everything is relative, and nutrition is part of the science of biology. Frequently nutrition is misunderstood, and sometimes it is exploited for untenable purposes by the ill-informed, but, generally speaking, its importance has gone unrecognized up to now. In such a context, the relationship between foodstuffs and the non-foods added to them (whether by accident or design) becomes of the utmost importance, as the work of Oltersdorf, Miltenberger and Cremer (1977) showed.

TOXICITY AND INDUCED EFFECTS CAUSED BY ALTERATIONS IN FOODS

Changes due to the intrinsic nature of the soil

The effect of the soil on the level of certain compounds found in foods has already been mentioned. In particular, it was seen that there is a connection between a lack of molybdenum in the soil and cancer of the oesophagus; this is caused by nitrosamines, which develop when the nitrates in the soil are not transformed owing to a lack in this trace element.

The excess of heavy metals found in plants, fish and certain animal products has also been mentioned. It is known that some areas are very rich in fluorine. A high level of fluorine can cause changes in the enamel of the teeth in both humans and animals living in the area, as has been reported from a small area of Greece, where the water contains 16 $\mu g/g$ of fluorine (A. Spaïs, personal communication). Similar effects have been noted in Argentina, Ireland, Italy, Morocco and the United States. Regarding this subject, mention should be made of the work done by Velu (1931) and Truhaut (1955).

In places where the soils are of glacial origin, Warren, Delavault and Fletcher (1971) noted multiple sclerosis of various organs among members of the population. The soils of these regions appear to contain lead, though not necessarily in quantities suitable for industrial use. Silver, barium and fluorine are also found. It is known that silver can alter the metabolism of tocopherol and thus promote the development of muscular dystrophy. There have been recent reports of natural lead-poisoning among Indian tribes of the Amazon.

According to Levina, Chekunova and Minkina (1973), lead may increase monoamine oxidase activity and cause, in rats, a progressive drop in certain of the organism's biogenic amines. The consequences are well known of these natural intakes, which are sometimes augmented by industrial pollution. However, pollution can be natural, producing either an excess of a harmful element in water or in plants or, through the reduction of the amount of an essential trace mineral element (e.g., a lack of molybdenum modifying the nutrition of plants), an increase in the concentration of a particular substance capable of harming the consumer[1]. What might be called "telluropathology" is the result of a geological imbalance. Although humans are less susceptible than animals to the direct effects of the nature of the soil, they still suffer indirectly as a consequence of changes in the

---

[1] An excess of molybdenum can, however, cause illness in bovines.

composition of plants, reduced harvests and the resulting constraint on animal production. It should be recalled that sulphur-containing glycosides can increase in crucifers after an application of fertilizer rich in sulphur and that goitrogenic plants are more harmful to people living in areas that lack iodine. Some crucifers may be inducers of cytochrome.

Schütte and Schendel (1958) have shown that, depending on the nature of the trace mineral element lacking in the soil, the level of various amino acids in a plant may be greatly modified. According to an anonymous article in *Nutrition Reviews* (1960), the vitamin content of turnips produced in some regions of Georgia (USA) is higher than in turnips of the same species produced in other parts of this State. The lack of phosphorus reduces the formation of proteins, sugars and starch in beans (Persanov and Andreeva, 1969). The effects of a lack of phosphorus are greater when the level of light is intensive. This lack may contribute to an increase in the levels of oestrogens in plants. It is obvious that climatic influences must also be taken into consideration, as they can play a very significant role in the variation of the composition of foods in a given element.

According to Maurice and Trocme (1965), the composition (particularly the mineral composition) of a plant when grown under identical conditions of soil and fertilizer is liable to vary considerably from year to year. Such variations are greater than those that result from varying degrees of soil fertility. This variability is more marked in the vegetative parts than in the seeds.

The general relationship between soil, plant, animal and man

As has been frequently stressed, there is a general soil/plant/animal/man relationship that varies slightly under climatic influences. It is not so absolute as was first thought since animals do not always react to changes in the same direction as plants nor man in the same direction as animals. All along these "links" there are antagonistic and synergistic effects taking place. Selenium and fluorine have no effect on plants but are harmful to animals. Molybdenum is favourable to plants but may, in excessive amounts, be harmful to animals, while its lack is dangerous to both.

These facts broaden the concept of "maximizing returns" and give it a more general biological meaning. They force us to look beyond the relationship between agricultural yields and economic returns in plant production and consider that there is a third important element in determining profits: the health of the consumer.

In the evolution of human nutrition, the speed of transportation and transfer between countries and continents makes it increasingly possible to offset local food deficiencies or imbalances that previously were caused by the area having to be strictly self-sufficient in food[1]. Unfortunately, this is not true for all countries. Autarky in food production is still too common a necessity in many areas. Not everywhere can variety in available foods offset a monotonous diet, the dangers of which are often increased by deficiencies or by dietary imbalances. Furthermore, growing numbers of unwary travellers, anxious to "get away from it all," become the victims of their love of the "natural" and the "exotic". In the industrialized countries, there are also dangers arising from food fads and fashions that can cause malnutrition either as a result of plain misinformation or by a deliberate exploitation of the naïve.

Effects on man of foods eaten by animals

The effects of animals eating foods that make them toxic to man, even though they themselves are not affected, need no long description. The case of the poisonous quail has already been mentioned. Snails, which quite rightly are starved before being eaten, can also transmit toxic substances to man while they themselves suffer no ill effects. Honey, too, especially that coming from exotic places, can turn out to be a medicinal honey with surprising properties. In ichthyism, which was discussed earlier, toxic effects can be caused by foods eaten by fish but which leave them unaffected. This is true for methylmercury. In the cases of the quail and ichthyism, the pollution was a natural process while, in the case of the mercury, there had been industrial pollution. This pollution was also the cause of casualties in pigs (Curley *et al.*, 1971) that had been carelessly fed on maize treated with a mercury salt. The flesh of these pigs was toxic to people who ate it.

According to Nevins and Grant (1971), the larvae of flies grown without any ill effect on composts containing aflatoxin transmit the poison to the trout that eat them. Luckily, however, the trout die and are not themselves eaten. It is also well known that aflatoxin passes into eggs and milk; ochratoxin also passes into the latter.

The reverse phenomena can also take place. Shrimps transform arsenic into organic compounds that are quickly eliminated from the organisms of mammals (Coulson, Remington and Lynch, 1935). Similar transformations take place with crayfish, lobster and other fish (Lund, 1972).

Such different behaviour comes within the framework of what Ferrando and Truhaut (1972a) called "relay toxicity", a term that covers both the

---

[1] As a result, goitre has almost disappeared from areas where, previously, it was endemic.

processes of detoxification and lethal synthesis. It is evident that changes brought about through a plant or an animal are chiefly a question of methodology relating to pesticides and additives present in animal feeds, but they also affect the quality of natural products, as further examples will show. These changes are still not very well understood and they would be worth a systematic study. They form part of a dynamic toxicology which, as is becoming increasingly evident, is closely linked to nutrition. Not all residues are used in the food chain.

Changes caused by preservation and storage

Changes can occur in foods during the processes used in preservation and storage. They are caused by chemical processes involving oxidation and Maillard reactions, which take place even at normal temperatures. These changes can also be caused by insects or moulds.

This collection of effects can bring about a reduction in nutritive value by changing or destroying essential nutritive elements. At the same time (or separately), bacterial contamination can come from insects, or from the formation of toxic substances by moulds.

The destruction and alteration of proteins during preservation, even at temperatures of around 30°C, are well known. Chichester (1973) examined the relationship between nutrition and methods of preparing or preserving food and reported that amino acids can be destroyed in proteins under conditions of severe heat treatment and that this can take place, more slowly, during storage in a warm atmosphere. Peptides and amino acids react more rapidly than proteins, among which there are differences in the rates of reaction.

The processes of degradation or alteration accelerate with rise in temperature and lowering in protein efficiency ratio of a food can thus be quite significant. Cooking bread at 232°C brings about a loss of 30 percent of the lysine added to wheat flour (Bender, 1966). This destruction, however, is limited to the bread crust.

Several authors think that preservation under poor conditions over a long period can prove to be harmful. Adrian and Favier (1961) have studied the behaviour of amino acids during the Maillard reaction. One of the important factors in this reaction is pH and the presence of carbohydrates increases the effects of degradation. Thus, the proteins in cereals, which are rich in carbohydrates, seem to be more sensitive to damage by heat or to prolonged storage under poor conditions, particularly in hot climates.

Oxygen uptake by unsaturated fatty acids of the lipids in foods causes these foods to be rancid. There are various kinds of rancidity:

- Hydrolytic rancidity of enzymatic origin;
- Ketonic rancidity caused by bacteria or moulds; these attack the short-chain fatty acids (C_4 to C_{14});
- Reversal, a phenomenon that is not yet fully understood, whereby an oil containing linoleic acid acquires a disagreeable odour and taste after being kept for some months;
- Rancidity by oxidation, or oxidative rancidity. This is the most common form and the most important from a nutritional and biological standpoint. It leads to the formation of peroxides, alcohols and ethylenic ketones and, finally, free radicals. In the course of these transformations, there are changes in taste and smell; destruction of essential polyunsaturated fatty acids, accompanied by changes to certain amino acids, methionine in particular, and to several vitamins: vitamin A and vitamin D, certain vitamins of the B complex and, of course, direct acceleration of the consumption of α-tocopherol (vitamin E) following the formation of free radicals; and perhaps, finally, there is an increased requirement for selenium, which is an activator of glutathione peroxidase.

We are beginning to learn more about the nutritional and metabolic consequences of these actions, particularly those produced at the cellular membranes and intracellular organelles, which lead to a variety of disorders that have been studied in domestic and laboratory animals. It has even been suggested that, in man, these changes could be one of the causes of ageing.

The action of insects and moulds adds to, and sometimes accelerates these physico-chemical processes of decay.

EFFECTS OF INSECTS

As this subject has already been dealt with in detail by several authors (Howe, 1965; Ferrando and Mainguy, 1970), a few examples will be given here of the changes brought about by insects.

According to Howe (1965), the global loss of foodstuffs, by weight, for which insects are responsible is estimated to be between 5 and 10 percent and could be even greater. Such losses are difficult to estimate because qualitative losses have to be added to quantitative losses; the former will be dealt with here. The rise in temperature caused by insects not only promotes their reproduction but increases the rate of physico-chemical degradation processes of nutrients (proteins, lipids, vitamins) and contributes to the development of harmful peroxides. This temperature increase can exceed 45°C. Insects limit their attacks to the cotyledons, germs and envelopes, i.e., to the richest parts of grains and seeds from a nutritional point of view. Yakovenko, Litvinov and Stoyanova (1973) have noted that wheat gluten loses a part of its physico-chemical properties as a result of the action of a certain parasite, the "cinch bug". In the particular variety in question, *Bezostaya* L., it is enough for 2 to 3 percent of the grain to be infected for the condition of the entire lot to be altered through enzymatic action. In other varieties the effect is less or even zero.

In six months, *Sitophilus oryzae* can bring about a nitrate loss of 25 percent. This insect, when it infests sorghum, causes a considerable increase in free fatty acids. In undamaged wheat the increase is normally between 19 and 37 mg of potash per 100 g of product. In a sample of wheat infested by three different types of insect, this increase can reach 44, and even 48 mg of potash per 100 g of product. The increase in rancidity is considerable, particularly in oily seeds. This action also brings about a reduction, if not the actual disappearance, of tocopherols and carotenoids in the grain or seed.

One of the most marked effects infestation has on wheat is the destruction of thiamine, the vitamin that is concentrated in the scutellum and the aleuronic layer. The loss of thiamine in non-infested wheat is very slight. In six months, the level decreases from 4.5 $\mu g/g$ to 4.2 $\mu g/g$. This loss increases considerably when the grain is infested by insects during storage. After six months only 2 $\mu g/g$ of thiamine may remain, or even less.

In sorghum infested by *Sitophilus oryzae*, thiamine decreases from 4.3 $\mu g/g$ to 2.9 $\mu g/g$, while the total weight loss is around 31.5 percent. The losses for rice are of the same order.

Kadkrol, Pingale and Swaminathan (1957) observed a lowering of thiamine content in groundnuts infested by *Corcyra cephalonica*. In six months, the level of this vitamin went from 10.8 $\mu g/g$ to 7.4 $\mu g/g$, while the control samples only lost 0.9 $\mu g/g$ in the same period.

Losses go up when the groundnuts are subsequently heated. Heating destroys vitamin B_1, while choline and lactoflavin are less affected. Several authors, quoted by Woodroof in his work on the groundnut (1966), state that the browner the oilcake the greater the loss in thiamine. This conclusion is logical, since the intensity of browning reflects the effect of heating. An increase in temperature caused by insects (which, as already mentioned, can reach more than 45°C) together with rancidity can cause the loss of other vitamins of the B complex, such as inositol and folic acid. Very probably the direct losses in other vitamins are similar to those for thiamine since the nutritional requirements of insects are not limited to vitamin B_1.

It has been suggested that there are toxic substances in the excreta of the parasitic insects found in grain, seed-flour and oilcake. These hepatotoxic substances cause the liver of the consumer to store vitamins and can thus have consequences that are much more serious than those provoked by a lowering of nutritive value, although the two actions could act synergistically.

EFFECTS OF MOULDS

The effects of moulds that develop during harvesting and storage are also harmful. These moulds can cause nutritive elements to disappear and even develop substances that have an antivitamin effect (Moreau, 1974). Nevertheless, Gorcica, Peterson and Steenbock (1935) noted that the development of moulds sometimes causes an increase in the vitamin content of the mouldy food. This is due to the high level of these substances in the mycelium. Thus *Aspergillus sydovi* seems to supply vitamins B_1, B_2 and other factors of the B complex. This enrichment can also affect protein content. Changes in amino acid balance are also liable to occur.

The most serious problem resulting from infestation by moulds is caused by the mycotoxins that they develop, which pass on toxic properties to food, either directly, when man comes to eat these foods, or, indirectly, by relay through an animal whose organism is not able to detoxify the substance or changes it into another harmful compound.

It is worth expanding a bit further on this question which, from some points of view, is highly topical. The grave health and economic consequences – as exemplified by the case of aflatoxin – are beyond dispute. Mycotoxins are not only a danger to health, they also act as a brake on the fight against protein deficiency just as they hinder agriculture and the general development of many countries. Arrhenius (1973) stated that mycotoxins represent an old health risk in a new dimension. They could not be described better.

What are mycotoxins?

Mycotoxins are metabolites, the chemical structures of most of which are known, produced by different varieties of fungi. They bring about abnormal and damaging biological changes in man, animals, plants and bacteria. The toxins can be contained in the spores or the thallus of the fungi, or secreted in the substrate on which they grow. The nature of the substrate can alter the nature of the toxin. When this substrate consists of cereals, oilseeds or other products eaten by man and animals, particular clinical signs may be observed following ingestion of infected foodstuffs.

In some parts of the world, moulds are used to give the rice, soybeans or fish a different flavour.

In France, a *Penicillium* is used in the manufacture of Roquefort cheese. The Bantu peoples of Africa consume numerous fermented preparations (Oettle, 1965). Beer made from sorghum has no aflatoxin when it is prepared under carefully controlled conditions, but that prepared in the home can be harmful to the drinkers.

Generally speaking, the dangers of contamination of human foodstuffs concern the populations of developing countries and, in particular, those countries in the tropical or equatorial areas. The hepatic damage observed following the consumption of mycotoxins can be compared with that seen in cases of prolonged administration of certain antibiotics such as triacetylo-leandomycin. It is also increasingly believed that protein undernourishment and lack of Vitamin A increase the effects of mycotoxins.

Toxins of fungal origin have been known for many years but in the past decade they have assumed a particular importance.

Numerous species of fungi besides moulds can develop toxins and bring about disturbances of varying degrees of seriousness, even to the point of being fatal.

Rye ergot, *Claviceps purpurea,* causes an illness that has been known since ancient times; it can contaminate flours used for bread making and produce toxic bread.

The death cap, *Amanita phalloides,* is hepatotoxic and, even if eaten in small amounts, causes death.

Many fungi are hallucinogenic and are used as such by certain tribes in Canada and in Mexico. But these fungi are easily visible and man has long learned to beware of them or to use them as drugs. This is not at all the case with moulds, which are not always visible or which can be dispersed, with their toxins, in mixed foods. Some of the diseases caused by moulds are mentioned below.

Alimentary toxic aleukia (ATA) is caused by eating grain infected with *Fusarium sporotrichoides* var. *tricinctum.* The toxin is produced on grain kept in the fields in winter. Joffe (1965) pointed out that this illness affects peoples who are undernourished. In 1944 it was widespread in the USSR, and it is still found there. Those affected show necrosis of the alimentary tract and other internal organs, accompanied by significant changes in the adrenal glands as well as inflammation of the skin. The fungus grows at zero-degree temperature and the toxin remains virulent even after storage for six or seven years.

Already in 1891, Sakaki recognized the predominant role of yellowed rice in the aetiology of certain kinds of beriberi. It was not until 1928 that Terauchi, Wada and Ohyama associated the occurrence of the disease brought on by eating yellowed rice with the presence of a toxin. This hypothesis was confirmed in 1940 when, in Taiwan, the consumption of stored rice (rice that had gone yellow) caused serious liver diseases and sometimes even death. More thorough research on such grain, particularly by Kraybill and Shimkin (1964), finally led to the demonstration of the presence of *Penicillium islandicum,* which produces several toxins (see Table 20) responsible for the symptoms observed in consumers of yellowed rice. Luteoskyrin, which is a mycotoxin metabolized by *P. islandicum* on rice, is, like islandicin, the cause of a primary liver cancer (Tatsuno, 1964).

Statistical evidence shows that the geographical areas in Asia where there is a high incidence of primary liver cancer in man are those where it is usual to eat yellowed rice.

Aflatoxins seem to be the most powerful liver carcinogens currently known. They are mainly metabolized by *Aspergillus flavus* and they are found especially on the seeds of plants that grow in tropical climates. The optimum condition for growth of the mould is a relative humidity of 80 percent at between 30 and 35°C. This explains why groundnuts, which are usually grown under these conditions, are so often affected. It would, however, be a mistake to think that only groundnut seed can be contaminated[1].

A systematic search for aflatoxins, carried out on various samples collected in markets in Thailand, shows that although groundnuts are the seeds most frequently contaminated, maize, millet, wheat, barley, soybeans and pepper can also be affected. In the markets of Hong Kong, haricot beans are the most contaminated; rice is rarely contaminated (Shank *et al.*, 1971, 1972). Aflatoxin has been found in material collected during the post-mortem examination of Thai children who died of acute encephalopathy with degeneration of the viscera (Shank *et al.*, 1971, 1972). In Uganda, Serk-Hanssen (1970) carried out an investigation following the death of a 15-year-old boy who showed centrolobular necrosis of the liver. Two young members of the same family had similar but less severe symptoms. The family store of cassava was found to contain 1.7 mg/kg of aflatoxins. Since it was not current practice in Uganda to carry out post-mortem anatomical or pathological studies, it is possible that the effect of the presence of aflatoxins on the mortality of the inhabitants of these regions may be greater than has been thought. It should also be noted that, according to Escher, Koehler and Ayres (1973), two toxin-producing strains of *Aspergillus ochraceus* have been isolated in ham in the United States.

Table 20, based on a publication by Genigeorgis and Riemann (1973), but slightly modified here, shows the main mycotoxicoses currently known in man.

Another possible form of poisoning by mycotoxins is through the consumption of the meat or the milk of animals that have ingested infected food in their rations. Small quantities of aflatoxin are found in chicken meat but the aflatoxin does not pass into eggs. However, it is transferred into milk, where the metabolite, milk aflatoxin, is found at a level of 1 percent of

---

[1] As regards edible oils, the refining processes eliminate aflatoxins and deodorization eliminates pesticide residues.

TABLE 20. Main mycotoxicoses currently known in man

Species	Foods infected	Toxins	Principal symptoms and lesions caused
Aspergillus flavus	Groundnuts, soybeans, haricot beans, cereal grain and by-products	Aflatoxins, milk aflatoxin	Hepatomas
Aspergillus ochraceus	Cereal grain, coffee, ham	Ochratoxins	(?)
Claviceps purpurea (rye ergot)	Cereal grain and by-products	Ergotine, ergotoxine, ergotamine, ergocristine, etc.	Ergotism (numbness of the extremities, convulsions, gangrene, etc.)
Fusarium graminearum and F. tricinctum	Cereal grain and by-products	Toxins of a complex nature, including zearalenone	Nausea, vomiting; oestrogenic action in pigs
Fusarium javanicum	Potatoes	–	Oedema of the lung in cattle
Fusarium sporotrichoides var. tricinctum [1]	Cereal grain and by-products, stone fruit	Fusariogenin	Alimentary toxic aleukia
Penicillium citroviride and P. citrinum	Rice	Citreoviridin, citrinin	Irritation of the skin and mucous membrane, toxicity to liver and kidneys
Penicillium cyclopium	Maize	Cyclopiazonic acid	(?)
Penicillium expansum	Apples, cider	Patulin	Carcinogenic, mutagenic
Penicillium islandicum	Rice	Icelandicin, icelanditoxin, rubroskyrin, enteoskyrin, erythroskyrin	Hepatotoxic, degeneration of the liver and hepatomas
Rhizopus nigricans	Coconut (tempeh)	–	Dizziness, convulsions, cyanosis (attributed to the consumption of tempeh in Java)
Stachybotrys atra	Vegetable debris, straw	Not isolated, very toxic	Dermatitis, catarrhal angina, leukopenia, action via the respiratory tract
Trichotecium roseum	Maize	Trichotecin and others	(?)

[1] Also *F. sporotrichiella*, according to Moreau (1974).

ingested aflatoxin. It seems that part of the milk toxin disappears after cold storage [1].

Considering the distribution of mycotoxins, and also the epidemiology of mycotoxicoses, the need to undertake measures to eliminate conditions liable to lead to their formation would appear urgent. It is well known that these fungal metabolites develop under certain conditions of humidity [2] and temperature.

There are three ways to combat the action of mycotoxins:

- Prevent the growth of the mould;
- Destroy the metabolites after their formation;
- Add a product to the foodstuff to eliminate the harmful action of the toxin or to enable the consumer's organism to detoxify it.

Climatic conditions contribute to fungal contamination, and the control of such conditions is one of the first steps in preventing mycotoxicoses. It is also the most important, since it is essentially preventive and there is no risk of altering the food or affecting the metabolism of the consumer.

Various effective procedures exist, especially for groundnuts, which can also be sorted to remove the toxic seeds. Another possibility is to improve storage conditions, which are, at present, poor.

A variety of processes have been put forward to detoxify groundnut and cotton oilcakes. The most effective, and the one that represents the least risk to the consumer, seems to be treatment with ammonia under pressure. This method is well established and most of the toxin is destroyed. An interesting point in this method is that the toxin continues to be eliminated during storage.

Studies on the effects of this treatment show that there is little or no change in nutritive values of foodstuff subjected to it.

The third solution is to add a product to the food that will inhibit the action of the mycotoxins. This has been studied in chickens. The addition of lysine and arginine diminishes a toxicity that is already of little importance in these animals. Trials have been carried out with enzyme inducers such as phenobarbital [3] but it is not yet known if the results will be convincing. It is obvious that this last procedure is the least satisfactory from the point of

---

[1] Observations made by N. Henry and the author in 1973 (not published). The milk/milk-aflatoxin complex is not harmful to ducks; it is not used in the food chain (Ferrando et al., 1977).

[2] At the request of WHO, an inquiry was undertaken into criteria of hygiene in the environment as regards mycotoxins.

[3] An antioxidant such as BHT also seems to be active.

view of the consumer's health since hepatic changes or imbalances in the diet can compromise its efficacy.

It is worth noting in closing that, if mycotoxins must bear some of the responsibility for primary liver cancers, they are certainly not the only cause. A careful study (Payet, 1965) has stressed the relationship between mycotoxicoses (at least, those due to *Aspergillus flavus*) and ecology. Payet (1965) also noted that tropical Africa has the unfortunate distinction of being the leading area for primary cancer of the liver. The Senegal river marks the northern limit for the distribution of liver cancer. In this region, where Senegalese and Moors are subject to the same ecological conditions, only black people, according to Payet (1965), are afflicted with this disease. It has also been found that cancer of the liver affects the black populations in the ratio of one woman to six men. Nevertheless, from the epidemiological data, a cause-and-effect relationship cannot be established between aflatoxins and liver lesions [1].

This brings the discussion back to the genetic basis of the predisposition to intolerance or allergies that was mentioned at the beginning of this study in connection with lactose and favism. The absence of certain enzymes, such as glucose-6-dehydrogenase in the case of favism, could explain the presence of these illnesses in one population category and the absence in another.

Just as there exists a geography of food and eating habits, there is also an ethnic variation in the possible reactions of consumers to a particular food. We are only now becoming aware of the role of genetics in pharmacodynamics.

Carcinogenic hydrocarbons

Carcinogenic hydrocarbons are found in some foods and in substances, peroxides in particular, that are formed during the preparation of food. Various polycyclic aromatic compounds suspected of being carcinogenic (1,2-benzanthracene, chrysene and others) are found in many common foods. The carcinogenic property of these substances is linked to certain electronic structures in their molecules, structures that lead to particular chemical reactions.

According to Fornal and Babuchowski (1970), as maize dried in the open matures, it develops carcinogenic substances such as 1,2- and 3,4-benzpy-

---

[1] Protein Advisory Group of the United Nations Organizations (PAG), *Report on the 19th meeting*, Geneva, 13-17 December 1971.

TABLE 21. Aromatic polycyclic compounds in various foods [1]
(µg/kg of fresh produce)

Source	3,4-benz-pyrene	1,12-benz-perylene	1,2,5,6-dibenzan-thracene	Reference
Salad	12.0	–	–	Gräf and Diehl (1966)
Spinach	12.0	–	–	” ”
Endive	50.0	–	–	” ”
Leek	6.6	4.2	0.2	Cahnmann and Kuratsune (1957)
Lettuce	150.0	–	–	Engst (1973)
Apple	0.1	–	–	”
Cod	15	–	–	Mallet, Perdrian and Perdrian (1963)
Mollusc (flesh)	55	–	–	” ”
Mollusc (shell)	18	–	–	” ”
Seaweed	60	–	–	” ”
Plankton	5.5	–	–	" ”

[1] No indication was given as to the state of the material used in the analysis.

rene in amounts of between 1.8 and 5.6 µg/kg. Further drying by artificial means can increase the amount of 3,4-benzpyrene.

According to Tilgner (1971), dangerous benzpyrenes are found not only in grain but also in bread, flour, cabbage, spinach, endives, etc. (see Table 21).

According to Shirotori and Takabatake (1973), there is no 3,4-benzpyrene in rice, fermented soybean paste (*miso*) and soy sauce, but 29.8 µg/kg can be found in dried bonito and 31.3 µg/kg in seafood. Engst (1973) also gives information on this subject. He examined the level of 3,4-benzpyrene in nine fruits and vegetables and found that apples contained 0.1 µg/kg of this compound and lettuce 150 µg/kg (see Table 21). Washing removed about 20 percent of the benzpyrene from apples leaving another 20 percent in the pulp. Humus contains 700 µg/kg of hydrocarbon. This figure would be lower in rural areas where there is little traffic, but it can go up to 3 000 µg/kg in industrial areas where traffic is heavy.

These compounds are also found in baking yeasts of various origin and, of course, in smoked food, such as the smoked fish and pork dishes that are so popular. Russian research workers (Dorogoplya *et al.*, 1972) have measured the level of one of these substances in dogs and in man after eating a meal of smoked sausages. Three hours after eating 1 kg of sausages containing 36 to 60 µg/kg of 3,4-benzpyrene, the lymph and the blood of the dog contained 0.01 to 0.014 µg and 0.0001 to 0.003 µg/ml respectively. Traces of benzpyrene were found in man following the consumption of 400 g of the same sausages. These levels are very low in relation to the amount of sausages involved, an amount that bears little relation to what would be eaten by the average person. According to these researchers, rats have to be left for 350 days in contact with the smoke of birch leaves, containing 0.04 to 0.17 µg of benzpyrene per m^3, before precancerous changes can be noted in the lungs, the digestive tract and the liver. The action of these compounds is quite localized and the organs are quite resistant to their effects. Petuely (1973) noted that the level of harmful compounds (anthracene, phenanthrene, pyrene, fluoranthene, chrysene, 1,2-benzanthracene and 3,4-benzpyrene) depends on the degree of smoking. The use of high temperatures during the smoke-curing process increases the levels of harmful compounds.

Smoke-curing has other, more immediate nutritional drawbacks. According to Chen and Issenberg (1972) it destroys up to 45 percent of lysine (an essential amino acid) in the meat and fish that are smoked. The cooking process brings about other changes, both harmful and beneficial [1]: Apart from the denaturation of proteins that takes place in food during heating, especially strong heating, one should also mention the compounds that are formed during frying, grilling, the skilful preparation of a *boeuf bourguignon* and, more generally, during the slow simmering of any tasty dinner.

Before talking about the effect of the cooking process on oils and fats, rape oil and erucic acid should be briefly considered. According to papers presented at a symposium held in April 1974 in Paris, at the Institut national de la santé et de la recherche médicale (INSERM), erucic acid that is present in rape oils seems to act like a foreign body in the cells of the myocardium [2]. It seems to be metabolized slowly. These results derive from

---

[1] For example, the effect on antitrypsins (see pages 23-29).
[2] See FAO. *Dietary fats and oils in human nutrition. Report of an Expert Consultation*, p. 46 *et seq.* Rome, 1977. FAO Food and Nutrition Paper No. 3.

TABLE 22. Effects of eating peroxidized fats on rats receiving suitable amounts of tocopherol (vitamin E)

Fat	Peroxide value	Peroxides in the ration ($\mu mol/g$)	Effect
Fish oil	50	10	No toxic effects (after 15 months, or 3 generations)
	775	70-80	Total depression of growth rate (after 5 weeks)
Soybean oil	600	10	No toxic effects
	600	40	Decrease in growth rate (by 30%)
	286	52	50% mortality rate in 2 weeks
	600	80	Total depression of growth rate
	600	120	Mortality of all subjects
Tallow	93	4-6	No toxic effects (after 6 weeks)
	258	52	Decrease in growth rate (by 18%)
Lard	200-300	20-30	Slight decrease in growth rate
Polyunsaturated fatty acids	1 461	80	Mortality of all subjects in 1 week

Source: Form various data collected by Lang (1970).
NOTE: The vitamin E requirement seems to have been underestimated.

in vitro studies. Over a prolonged period, the mortality rate in rats fed on these oils was not unusually high. However, under heat stress, the mortality rate increases when olive oil is substituted for rape oils in the diet. Mortality depends on the level of erucic acid in the oil. The following relationships between oils exist as regards mortality:

Olive oil < Cambra oil (a rape oil lacking erucic acid) < Rape oil

In 1970, Lang carried out an extensive review of the effects of cooking on food. In particular, he listed the substances that develop during the reaction between sugars and proteins (Maillard reaction). This reaction has already been mentioned in connection with the possible changes that can occur during storage, but changes are more significant during heating to high temperatures.

Lang also examined the effect on rats of eating foods fried in plain fat and in peroxidized fats. With plain fat the results are not very clear while, with peroxidized fats, they are more clear-cut, although they vary greatly according to the nature of the fats and their level of peroxides (see Table 22).

So there is much to reflect upon and plenty could still be said about the products of the Maillard reaction, peroxides, and the aromatic polycyclic compounds in smoked meat and pork products. Something that comes to mind immediately is the current fashion of cooking on a barbecue. This is an ideal method of forming benzpyrenes, peroxides and other compounds that have been shown to be harmful in tests carried out under experimental conditions. Some of these aromatic polycyclic compounds are also enzyme inducers.

When the possible toxicity of non-stick coatings on certain kitchen utensils is discussed, it is often forgotten that the products of the breakdown of fats used to grease equivalent, but not non-stick, utensils can be equally dangerous. Has anyone ever systematically studied the degree of possible danger in these cases? In more general terms, it is worth mentioning a wry observation made during a discussion on the possible harmful effects of preserving foodstuffs by radappertization (irradiation treatment): "If we had never known about fire and it were suddenly discovered now, certain people, on learning of the possible harmful consequences it can have on food, would be clamouring for its prohibition."

Conclusions

Readers have seen how many toxic substances are naturally present in the most everyday foods eaten by man. They have also seen the difficulties involved in determining the inner processes that are at the basis of the illnesses they cause, in isolating the causative elements and, finally, in finding a direct or indirect means of neutralizing them. Sometimes, even though there is no means of doing so, the plant concerned continues to be cultivated. For example, even though lathyrism has been known in India and in Mediterranean countries for a long time, plants of the genus *Lathyrus* continue to be grown. In some regions, the disease becomes endemic. It is odd to see how many natural condiments have, after long years of usage followed by a short test, been declared toxic. Apart from alcohol and cigarettes, there are many other toxic substances. F.J. Stare (1969), Professor of Nutrition at Harvard, was correct when he said that high-calorie diets rich in saturated fatty acids, cholesterol and sugars lead to a nutritional imbalance as a result of the various excesses.

The multiple consequences on human health resulting from such excesses, or from such unbalanced dietary habits, are all the more serious in that this kind of malnutrition is accompanied by the variety of stresses implicit in modern living. Among these should be included consumers' concern for the unknown effects of the food they eat. There is a certain type of journalism that likes to play on these fears by threatening consumers with a variety of evils that can befall them as a result of the use of certain modern agricultural techniques, but without which they would almost certainly go hungry. Nothing is ever said about natural foods since it is axiomatic to all (except nutritionists and specialists in toxicology) that whatever is natural is good for you.

What would be the result, one wonders, if the same care and expense as are now normally devoted to studies on non-traditional foods prepared by new methods (or on new additives for human and animal foods) were to be lavished on a study of the harmful effects of man's traditional foods?

Adapting the words Beaumarchais put into Figaro's mouth regarding masters and servants, so that they apply to natural foods on the one hand, and to non-traditional foods and additives on the other, one can say: considering the qualities demanded of a non-traditional food or an additive, there are very few natural foods that would be worthy of being one or the other. Happily, however, there is no danger of such negative scrutiny, since greed, habit, tradition and myths concerning food (and sometimes, unfortunately, plain need) will all unite to prevent such standards being applied; we should be thankful for this. Since, indeed, the pleasures of the table have contributed in no small way to the development of a type of civilization that it would be a pity to see jeopardized or to vanish altogether, one should expose and fight against those fanatics — or, worse still, those exploiters of the "natural" — the victims of and profiteers from a real syndrome of "pollutionitis."

However, it is still useful to investigate more closely the harmful substances found in natural foods and to find the means of alleviating their effects, either by the selection of non-toxic varieties, or through using technical or culinary processes capable of destroying them. Populations that are, or could be, endangered by eating natural foods that are liable to contain harmful substances should be educated and informed about nutrition. Equally, it would be worth educating the general public about the benefits of the progress made in agriculture and to demonstrate (as can easily be done) that without such progress the world would still be suffering from the famines of years ago.

Part Two

NON-TRADITIONAL FOODS

NON-TRADITIONAL NUTRITION

Introduction

International supply shortages in the period between May and August 1973 showed just how precarious the supply is of soybean protein in Europe, where it is used as animal feed and thus, indirectly, as human food. Population growth in many countries, combined with a rising standard of living, has led to increased shortages of protein and energy and, more generally, to a lack of balanced foods.

Great hopes were aroused by the "green revolution," the high point of which seems to have occurred in 1967. In Asia, the use of new or improved varieties of wheat and rice had led to an enormous increase in the number of hectares sown with these two cereals: the 1 638 000 hectares sown in 1966/67 had become 17 773 000 hectares by 1969/70. This does not, however, seem to be enough, since the gains of agricultural progress are gradually being nullified by demographic changes.

In the Punjab, the Ludhiana district quadrupled its wheat production in six years, getting yields of 60 quintals to the hectare as a result of using new varieties. Nevertheless, in order to achieve these results the district used 20 times as much fertilizer in 1972 as it did in 1962. The number of tractors had to be increased considerably and irrigation had to be greatly expanded. The use of these new varieties of cereals − upon which the green revolution is based − demands more investment and fertilizer to achieve the maximum returns [1]. They are also more susceptible to disease than the more common varieties used previously. The increase in the use of fertilizer in Asia, compared with previous years, was 3 percent for 1964/65. It went up to 22 percent between 1966 and 1968, and dropped back to 7 percent in 1968/69 at (or even slightly below) which level it has remained in subsequent years.

---

[1] Even so, these new varieties themselves give higher yields than the local varieties. But the overall costs in energy for these crops is, unfortunately, higher.

The investments required to ensure increased grain production are quite considerable. They involve not only fertilizer but also irrigation, roads and storage facilities. The rational exploitation of new varieties of cereals can only be carried out correctly if sufficient capital is made available. Finally, despite the use of mutant strains of maize, such as 'Opaque-2' and 'Floury-2', these new cereals are not perfect sources of proteins.

The first obstacle to the development of new types of food is a certain conservative spirit, which frequently is nothing more than the reflection of a lack of imagination or of a profound intellectual laziness. Then there is the plain suspicion with which people regard foods that are not their traditional foods. But quite apart from any psychological factors involved, this distaste is also caused by an ignorance of the origin and composition of these foods and their value as a supplement to traditional foods. In this section, these foods will be examined; it will be stressed, however, that before they are used as food for humans, they can be extremely useful as animal feeds, thus demonstrating their safety and efficacy while supplying human consumers with high-quality proteins in the form of meat, milk and eggs.

Bearing in mind the above reservations, the possibilities that this field offers include:

- The development of oilseed crops and of the proteins extracted from their seeds for utilization as protein sources;
- The extraction of protein (generally known as leaf protein [1]) from plants such as alfalfa, clover, leaves;
- The utilization (initially as animal feed) of new substrates in growing single-cell or multi-cell organisms rich in high-quality protein. These substrates include: gas oil; normal paraffins; methyl alcohol and other alcohols; latex serum of the Para rubber tree; cereals, roots, tubers and straw; liquids recovered from starch and potato starch factories; and pig dung and other excrements and effluent. This list is only indicative and could be much longer.

Crop development and the use of food protein sources will not be examined here, since the means of expanding crops is outside the scope of this book and since, because these are traditional foods, their various aspects have already been dealt with. However, attention will be paid to proteins extracted from grasses and other plant leaves, alfalfa in particular, and to the use of new substrates for the growing of single- and multi-cell organ-

---

[1] This term does not imply that the proteins are extracted only from the leaves of herbaceous plants. Very often the whole plant is used, as in the cases of alfalfa and clover.

isms. The latter is a more complex subject. At present, this source of protein can be considered only in relation to animal feed (at least as regards protein from single- or multi-cell organisms), since proteins extracted from grasses already present problems in animal feeding.

Finally, the possibilities will be examined of preparing truly non-traditional foods for humans by using protein concentrates extracted from leguminous plants, grasses, leaves and, probably in the future, yeasts grown on new substrates. A whole range of substrates could be employed, ranging from cellulose waste to animal waste, to supply protein and, at the same time, to prevent wastage and pollution while freeing land for new crops. In this domain, imaginative research workers could come up with techniques to allow for a variety of solutions.

Proteins extracted from various seeds

At present, only proteins obtained from leguminous plants, mainly soybeans (but also sunflowers, peas and field beans), are used in the preparation of non-traditional foods. In several countries, particularly France and the countries of Eastern Europe, efforts have been made to use rapeseed, but here it is essential first to remove the antithyroid substances that are present. There are various industrial processes to do this. Sims (1971) and Lo and Hill (1971) describe some of them. However, Eklund (1973) was not satisfied with the results observed when he fed the detoxified protein concentrate to female rats: two out of seven rats produced foetuses of below-average size and the survival rate was highly unsatisfactory.

Bacteria and moulds were used by Poznanski et al. (1973) to detoxify rape flour. *Byssochlamys fulva* and *Penicillium chrysogenum* destroy 3-butenylisothiocyanate. *B. fulva* and *Bacillus helveticus* also destroy this compound, as well as 5-vinyl-2-thiooxazolidone. The actions of *B. helveticus* and *Escherichia coli* have also been combined to attack these two toxic compounds. Microorganisms can completely hydrolyse compounds with SCN^- groups. The detoxification is accompanied by an increase in the level of proteins (41.90 percent as against 31.00 percent). These proteins are richer in lysine. It would be more effective to select rape varieties that do not contain goitrogenic compounds, as was done in the case of erucic acid (cambra). According to Morice (1970), this possibility exists. The seeds of the Polish 'Bronowski' rape only contain traces of the thioglucosides that are of medical concern: a content of 1 percent, as against 5-16 percent in spring rape and 6-19 percent in winter rape. Special methods of cross- and backbreeding, followed by selection, should lead to the production of varieties that are almost totally free of goitrogenic compounds. As regards the isolation of proteins from rape, this would put us in a position similar to that attained for soybeans; and, as regards the preparation of non-traditional foods, in conditions that will be examined at the end of this second section.

Proteins extracted from leaves

Interest in extracting foodstuffs from leaves (leaf protein) goes back a long time. Already in 1773, i.e., 65 years before the discovery of proteins, Rouelle, Professor of Chemistry at the Jardin des Plantes in Paris, mentioned the presence in plants of "glutenous or plant/animal substance." In 1924 and 1925, patents were registered in Hungary and the United Kingdom for the extraction of protein from plants.

But are the proteins extracted from plants and leaves really useful and can they be produced on an industrial scale?

Oelshlegel, Schroeder and Stahmann (1966) have stressed that cows only transform 10-15 percent of the vegetable proteins they eat into animal proteins. Theoretically, therefore, the ideal solution would be to extract and concentrate the proteins from the leaves and fodder in order to avoid such wastage. Cheeke and Myer (1973) believe that alfalfa could be treated in this way. This fodder plant produces a large amount of protein per hectare. In favourable conditions the figure for protein production can be 4 to 5 tons or even more.

Proteins can also be obtained from aquatic plants (Boyd, mentioned in Pirie, 1971). Boyd cites such plants as *Nymphaea odorata, Brasenia schreberi* and *Nelumbo luteo* as being capable of supplying 1 800, 790 and 990 kg of fresh plants per hectare respectively. *Justicia americana* and *Alternanthera philoxeroides* also give very high yields (24 580 and 7 980 kg/ha respectively, according to Boyd [1969]). About 25 percent of the total nitrogen can be extracted from these aquatic plants.

Research into the preparation of protein concentrate began around 1940 in the United Kingdom and the United States. The various stages of development will not be discussed here but mention should be made of the work of Festenstein (1961), and especially of Morrison and Pirie (1961), who perfected the techniques, along with Henry and Ford (1965), who also took part in these studies. The work of Hollò (1969) in Hungary should be noted, as well as that of the present author (although research was begun in 1958, the results were only published much later), the work of Canadian researchers referred to later (1971) and, finally, the work of Yasui and Iwamatsu (1972). These studies all have points in common between them even though they were carried out independently. The general system of preparation involves the following steps:

- Crushing: this should produce as fine a result as possible;
- Pressing to extract the juice: various processes can be applied;
- Precipitation or coagulation of the proteins by a variety of methods, followed by washing, decolorization, drying and concentration.

In addition to protein concentrate (leaf protein), a cake rich in cellulose is obtained, which can be used as feed for ruminants, as well as a clear juice that, according to studies, is an excellent substrate for the cultivation and development of yeasts.

The amino acids of 20 raw preparations of proteins from leaves and plants have been analysed by Pirie (1969), who compared them with the recommended values published by FAO (1965).

Amino acid	Range	Recommendation[1]
	(g of amino acid/100 g of protein)	
Isoleucine	4.7- 5.2	4.2
Leucine	8.8-10.0	4.8
Lysine	5.6- 7.1	4.2
Methionine	1.7- 2.8	2.2
Cystine	(2)	2.0
Phenylalanine	5.5- 6.4	2.8
Threonine	4.8- 5.7	2.8
Tryptophan	1.7- 2.3	1.4
Tyrosine	3.9- 4.6	2.8
Valine	6.0- 7.2	4.2

[1] FAO (1965).
[2] The value for cystine is not certain, but is around 1.

Pirie (1969) considers that leaf proteins can supplement nitrogen in diets poor in protein to an extent at least equal to that of most seeds. Equivalent figures for alfalfa concentrates are given in Table 23. All researchers noted the lack of methionine in these concentrates. This deficiency exists in other foods, but it is not a matter for concern since DL-methionine is synthesized on a large scale and, consequently, is available at low cost.

A series of experiments on rats studied the protein efficiency ratio (PER) of concentrates prepared in the laboratory from alfalfa. The PER results (averages) were as follows: 1.27 for alfalfa decolorized by the Spray process, 1.55

**TABLE 23. Essential amino acids in alfalfa-protein concentrates
and in egg: determination of chemical score**

(g of amino acid/100 g of protein)

Amino acids	Dried protein concentrate from alfalfa		Whole egg
	Spray process	Hatmaker process	
Arginine	6.9	5.2	6.4
Histidine	2.7	1.9	2.1
Lysine	6.1	5.3	7.2
Tyrosine	5.0	3.7	4.5
Phenylalanine	7.2	5.6	6.3
Methionine	1.9	1.2	4.1
Threonine	6.6	5.3	4.9
Leucine	9.8	7.5	9.2
Isoleucine	6.3	4.4	8.0
Valine	7.1	6.3	7.3
Limiting factor	Methionine	Methionine	
Percentage of deficiency ..	53.6	70	–
Chemical score	46.4	30	–

Source: Based on studies carried out by the author.

for the same product supplemented with 0.3 percent of DL-methionine and 0.67 for a concentrate dried by the Hatmaker process (i.e., superheating followed by depigmentation).

If one compares these three values to the protein efficiency ratio of casein supplemented by 0.3 percent of DL-methionine and to other sources of protein, the following results are obtained:

Casein + 0.3 percent of DL-methionine	100 (reference standard)
Casein alone	76
Protein extracted from Spray-depigmented alfalfa ..	52
Protein extracted from Spray-depigmented alfalfa + 0.3 percent of DL-methionine	64
Protein extracted from Hatmaker-depigmented alfalfa	22
Yeasts cultivated on alkanes	77- 85
Yeasts cultivated on alkanes + 0.3 percent of DL-methionine	97-106
Soybean flour (cooked)	95

The reference standard (100) was established by using the average of the figures obtained in the laboratory, i.e., 2.41 (1.93 to 2.89). The same was done for casein not supplemented by 0.3 percent of DL-methionine. This figure is close to that generally given for casein, (2.5), while the classic value for soybeans is 1.80.

Depigmentation of the protein extracted from alfalfa is considered essential. In trials carried out with rats and chickens, the effects of products that had not been depigmented always led to the death of some of the animals when the concentrates were used to supply 13 or 10 percent of the diet as the only source of proteins. The protein efficiency ratio varied, in these conditions, between 0.37 and 0.89. Partial depigmentation gave a protein efficiency ratio of 1.34 without, however, preventing some mortality. The spray-dried juice already has a food value inferior to that of precipitated protein (Ferrando and Spaïs, 1966). As well as serum, it seems essential to eliminate certain harmful substances, referred to by Lepkovsky *et al.* as early as 1950, that Olson, Pudelkiewicz and Matterson (1966) believe hasten the elimination of tocopherol. It is quite likely that these vegetable-protein extracts contain other harmful elements similar to those found in the seeds of certain legumes. This would explain the following values (*Nutrition Reviews*, 1972) of the protein efficiency ratio of leaf proteins:

> nil for 5 plants
> < 1.0 for 6 plants
> > 1.75 for 5 plants

According to Cheeke and Myer (1973) the partial use of these concentrates (in amounts of between 6.5 and 13 percent of the diet) gives good results. Hove *et al.* (1974), while emphasizing the ability of alfalfa-protein extracts to cause photosensitization in the rat, showed that when these constitute only 10 percent of the diet there are no harmful effects on growth, reproduction or on the offspring compared with a diet based on casein. Supplementary sulphur-containing amino acids should always be given. However, when used in amounts of 20 to 30 percent of the diet, a slowdown in growth is noted, which also seems considerably inhibited by the serum of alfalfa collected after precipitation of the proteins. Canadian research workers (Tao *et al.*, 1972) have, however, obtained decolorized leaf proteins without a disagreeable taste by means of a special extraction process, and with a protein efficiency ratio of around 2.

The international symposium report edited by Pirie (1971) contains a paper by Singh concerning the favourable results obtained on children by Doraiswamy *et al.* (including Singh, 1969). The tests were carried out over a

TABLE 24. Nitrogen retention in children recovering from malnutrition

Diet	Milk	Leaf protein	Milk	Leaf protein
Number of tests	11	5	10	5
Amount given (mg/kg/day)	776	765	504	496
Amount retained (mg/kg/day)	276	246	165	160

NOTE: The children were fed diets containing milk as the only source of nitrogen and diets where half of the milk was replaced by leaf proteins.

long period using concentrates of alfalfa shoots prepared by a method conceived by Davys and Pirie (1963). The results are given in Table 24.

The figures in the table show that good balances are obtained. These data confirm those of Waterlow (1962), who used such concentrates in Jamaica with children suffering from kwashiorkor. In a balanced diet of fats, carbohydrates, vitamins and trace mineral elements, the proteins were supplied first in the form of skim milk. Then the diet continued with between 57 and 74 percent of the milk proteins being replaced by proteins extracted from the leaves of maize or wheat. The daily gain in weight by the children is similar for both these extracts, while the milk proteins give a slightly better growth rate. A comparison of the nitrogen absorption in the two cases shows 5.4 percent greater nitrogen absorption on milk proteins. The difference, therefore, is slight.

Studies on man have only just begun, but the initial results are encouraging. Machines that prepare protein concentrates from leaves or grasses are now operating in Europe, Jamaica, India and are ready for use in Uganda and New Guinea. These are all pilot plants, except for a factory in Hungary and another in Spain (in Lerida province).

It should be carefully stressed, however, that before concentrates can be utilized, any toxic substances that they contain must first be removed and extra amino acids added, especially sulphur-containing amino acids, as well as any other substance that may be lacking.

The final use to which these proteins are to be put, and the economics and psychology of their use, should always be borne in mind. As Pirie (1971) has pointed out, the introduction of leaf proteins to the dining table presents some problems. He gives a few recipes, including ones for:

● Potato, onion and leaf-protein paste;
● Leaf-protein vegetable stew;
● Fish, cabbage and leaf-protein paste.

Pirie gives all the instructions required to make a series of mixtures that, although nourishing, would make a gourmet shudder. Nevertheless, the possibility of preparing completely decolorized protein from leaves and grasses will certainly contribute to the enrichment of sources of non-traditional foods, which are discussed at the end of this second section. The problem is not an easy one. In some foodstuffs, even though they are extracted from natural products, there is a whole series of substances that are still completely unknown or very little known.

The Protein Advisory Group of the United Nations (PAG [1]) has stressed these various drawbacks, particularly those relating to colour, taste and, sometimes, the lack of product stability. Nevertheless, Bickoff and Kohler (1973), writing in *PAG Bulletin*, have pointed out that the use of the by-products remaining after the extraction of decolorized protein from alfalfa in animal fodder would reduce the cost price. This hypothetical concentrate could contain, according to these writers, up to 90 percent of the crude protein value (cpv). According to the norms established by FAO, the average daily requirement per person can be estimated at 35 g; if one accepts the above hypothesis, then the protein requirement of twice the world's present population could be satisfied by growing alfalfa on a surface area equal to the size of Texas. Bickoff and Kohler (1973) have remarked that in the residues of alfalfa there is enough protein for it to be dehydrated or ensiled and then used as cattle fodder to produce extra milk and meat. However, production costs and consumer tastes have to be borne in mind as well.

Proteins from single- or multi-cell organisms

Among the primary protein-rich non-traditional foods, careful attention should be given to single- or multi-cell organisms, which are cultivated on a variety of different substrates.

Although relatively small quantities of these organisms are currently produced, interest in them continues to grow because of the role they could play in the future as foodstuffs. Several writers, including Sénez (1972, 1973) and Kihlberg (1972), have studied the consequences of this development.

---

[1] PAG. *Leaf protein concentrate*, 11 June 1970, Report No. 11. On 1 January 1978, PAG was replaced by a new body consisting of a Sub-Committee on Nutrition (SCN) of the UN Administrative Coordination Committee, with technical support from the Advisory Group on Nutrition (AGN).

Numerous substrates are used for these cultures: latex serum of the Para rubber tree (which, as was demonstrated in 1957, can be distributed directly to animals), whey, molasses, by-products from starch and potato-starch factories, the residual juice after the proteins have been extracted from alfalfa and other plants, as well as grain, straw and various agricultural wastes. Even excrement can be used, according to patents filed by Stevens and Harmon (1970, 1972). Cellulose waste-matter found in both city and country can, after being finely chopped, treated with soda, heated between 20 and 100°C and then neutralized, serve as a substrate and supply energy to aerobic and anaerobic fermentation and produce a biomass that, after drying, contains 60 percent of CPV (*Chem. Engng News*, 1974b).

At present, however, the substrates receiving the most attention are alkanes and methanol. The potential production of single-cell proteins starting from alkanes is around 20 million tons, i.e., the protein equivalent of the world's rice or soybean crop.

The biomasses obtained from these cultures have already been the subject of numerous tests, initially toxicological, and then zootechnical. They have also occasioned many unfounded assertions and tendentious newspaper articles. It is important, therefore, to examine them more carefully by looking at their composition, the foreign elements they are liable to contain, and their nutritive value, in the light of the numerous results of experiments that have already been carried out in animal breeding. Their future as human food is linked to these different data.

The microorganisms cultivated on different substrates can be grouped as follows:

● Food yeasts (*Saccharomyces, Torula, Candida*), which are well known and have been in use for a long time. They will not be discussed here. World production of these yeasts is around 350 000 tons. They are grown on classic substrates such as sugar, starch, lactoserum, molasses and sulphited liquids. The fact that they have been used for so long has, paradoxically, exempted them from being studied and appraised systematically and thoroughly. Tradition and habit account for a lot.

● Moulds (*Fusarium, Penicillium notatum*), which are grown on starch, the production of which has not developed very much. Furthermore, the tendency now is to use filamentous fungi.

● Algae (*Chlorella, Schenedesmus* and *Spirulina*), which have been studied for the past 20 years in the United States and (particularly *Chlorella*) in Japan; *Scenedesmus* has been studied in Italy and the blue algae, *Spirulina maxima*, in Chad, France and Mexico.

● Yeasts of the genus *Candida* (*tropicalis* or *lipolitica*), which are grown on alkanes.

● Bacteria that are grown on methanol or hydrocarbons (*Methanomonas* and *Pseudomonas*).
● Filamentous fungi, which are grown on cereals, cassava, etc.

In a meeting on 13 and 14 December 1973, PAG recalled that the term "single-cell protein" had been selected in 1966 as the title for the first international conference organized on this subject. It was considered a new and sufficiently neutral term, which would avoid the connotations of microbial protein, bacterial protein and, above all, petroleum protein.

Proteins derived from bacteria, yeasts, moulds and algae can, thus, be called single-cell proteins even though the name is not an accurate description of these materials, since some of them are not monocellular at all. Apart from proteins, these organisms also contain carbohydrates, lipids, nucleic acids, vitamins and minerals. Thus, in addition to proteins, they also ensure an intake of energy and other nutrients.

In view of the differences in the levels of proteins and amino acids, and differences in their digestibility, nutritive values and toxicological properties, distinctions should be made between them. However, it is difficult to find a more suitable term for labelling and standard-setting purposes.

It was suggested by PAG [1] that a term, or terms, should be chosen to serve as a basis for a nomenclature that would identify the two types of microorganisms and the substrates upon which they are produced. These terms would not be substituted for the manufacturers' individual brand names but they would help the public to see that single-cell proteins can be as different from each other as are fruit, vegetables, meats and fish.

Such a system of nomenclature would not only be a source of information for technicians, administrators and consumers, but would also have an advantage over other terms such as petroleum proteins or bacterial proteins. PAG felt that if a nomenclature free from adverse connotations were not adopted, the acceptance of single-cell proteins, and the success of producing and commercializing such a useful source of food, could be compromised as a result of misunderstandings by the consumer.

So far, apart from a few exceptions such as algae and, of course, yeasts that are considered to be classic, studies have mainly centred on the food value of yeasts and bacteria grown on alkanes and methanol. It is clear that, in keeping with the PAG (1971) recommendations, these new foods should at least have the same, if not a higher, food value than that of products normally used in the feeding of domestic animals. Two criteria have been proposed:

---

[1] In a symposium on this question held in Brussels in 1975.

● The products should be sufficiently standardized and constant in composition;

● The biomass should not contain any toxic substance liable to affect the health of the consumer, either via the organism of a farm animal, in the first instance, or later, when used directly.

Chemical analyses and zootechnical tests can ensure compliance with these points. It should be stressed that these analyses and tests already provide significant assurances in the evaluation of non-traditional foods with a view to using them directly as human food.

One observation should be made, which was formulated at a meeting of the PAG in 1975 by experts, and with good reason.

It did not seem logical to consider that every product derived from microorganisms was inedible by man and animals just because some of them are toxic. If this reasoning were carried to the extreme it could also be applied to plants and mushrooms. It is better simply to make a distinction between what is good and what is bad. For traditional foods this selection was arrived at empirically, slowly and imperfectly. For non-traditional foods, the selection should be done on a scientific basis and be accurate and quick.

The compositions of some of these non-traditional foods in essential amino acids, expressed for 16 g of nitrogen, are shown in Table 25. Some figures have been taken from a work by Sénez (1972) and the rest from other data.

As in Sénez (1972), the various levels of amino acids in the selected non-traditional foods have been compared here with those in whole egg, with FAO standards and with two commonly used foodstuffs added to animal feed: herring fish-meal and soybean cake.

A comparison of the figures in the table shows that single- and multi-cell organisms are extremely rich in good-quality proteins and that their level of heavy metals and polycyclic aromatic compounds is extremely low. Table 26 (previously published by Ferrando in 1972) presents some results of analyses carried out in the laboratory of Professor Grimmer. Recent data obtained by Bories and Tulliez (1973) and Faugère (personal communication) have been added. These results also refer to classic yeasts; they have recently been confirmed.

A look at the figures in Table 26 shows how even the most classic of yeasts, grown on conventional substrates, are richer in aromatic polycyclical compounds than yeasts grown on alkanes. It is also known that oysters can contain hydrocarbons. Such is the case, for example, of those found in Galveston Bay, near Houston, and in the approach canal to shore installations provided for oil tankers. It has already been pointed out (page 70) that

TABLE 25. **Essential amino acids contained in selected non-traditional foods** [1]

(g / 100 g of crude protein)

Amino acid	Whole egg	FAO standard	Soybean cake [2]	Herring fish-meal [2]	Brewer's yeast [2]	Yeast, France [3]	Yeast, UK [3]	Yeast [4]	Yeast [5]	Yeast [6]	Yeast [7]	Bacteria [8]	Cyano-phyceae [9]
Isoleucine	8	4.2	5.10	4.7	5.85	5.3	5.05	4.70	4.3	3.28	5.28	4.3	4.8
Leucine	9.2	4.8	7.90	7.4	8.00	7.8	7.40	8.18	6.8	3.75	7.90	6.3	6.1
Lysine	7.2	4.2	6.60	4.8	9.05	7.8	7.40	7.03	5.9	4.52	10.03	5.4	6.1
Phenylalanine	6.3	2.8	5.40	3.1	4.85	4.8	4.30	4.10	3.4	2.62	4.59	4.1	4.9
Threonine	4.9	2.8	4.05	4.3	5.50	5.4	4.85	5.11	4.6	3.06	5.50	4.0	4.0
Tyrosine	4.5	2.8	4.00	1.9	4.15	4.0	3.60	3.56	3.1	1.98	4.04	3.1	3.5
Histidine	2.1	–	2.75	1.5	2.50	2.1	2.10	2.77	–	1.33	1.88	–	–
Valine	7.3	4.2	5.50	5.7	7.35	5.8	5.80	5.90	5.6	3.27	5.84	4.9	5.0
Methionine	4.1	4.2	4.15	1.1	1.60	1.6	1.80	1.70	2.4	0.73	1.51	2.6	2.9
Cystine	2.4			0.6	0.90	0.9	1.10	0.86	0.6	1.06	1.10		
Arginine	6.4	–	7.60	7.2	5.00	5.0	5.10	7.03	4.5	2.72	4.45	–	–
Tryptophan	1.5	1.4	–	–	–	1.3	1.40	0.97	0.9	0.73	1.00	0.8	1.3
CPV (N × 6.25) (g/100 g of foodstuff)	–	–	52	78.5	47.8	72	70	62	80	60	56	60	[10] 54-80

[1] *Sénez* (1972) and the present author. – [2] Pion and Fauconneau (1966). – [3] *Candida tropicalis* grown on alkanes (BP registration records, France and United Kingdom). – [4] Other yeast grown on N-paraffins. – [5] Yeast prepared by Imperial Chemical Industries. – [6] Liquipron. *Candida* on N-paraffins. – [7] Yeast grown on alkanes (Esso-Nestlé; Mauron, 1969). – [8] *Micrococcus* sp. grown on alkanes. – [9] *Spirulina maxima* (Institut français du pétrole; Giddey and Menzi, 1967). – [10] Depending on culture process, drying and after 80-percent decolorizing.

TABLE 26. Polycyclic aromatic compounds found in selected yeasts
(μg/kg of dry matter)

Source	3,4-benzpyrene	1,12-benzpyrene	1,2,5,6-dibenz-anthracene
"La Parisienne" baker's yeast (origin: Epernon)	12.2	4.3	0
"St. Louis" baker's yeast (origin: Marseilles)	8.0	3.8	0
"Gayelord Hauser" special dietary "superyeast" (origin: Epernon)	0	0	0
German baker's yeast "Deutsche Hefe" (origin: Hamburg)	13.2	9.7	0
"Deutsche Hefe" special dietary German baker's yeast (origin: Hamburg)	0	0	0
Russian industrial yeast (origin: "Le Francois", Paris)	8.7	6.0	0
BP yeast (origin: Lavera)	0.55	0	0.1
BP yeast (origin: Grangemouth)	2.5	1.3	0.5
ELF, ERAP yeast (origin: Lyon-Solaize)	<1; same level for benzo-K-fluoranthrene and 20-methylcholanthrene		

some common vegetables such as endives, leeks, lettuce and spinach contain levels of 3,4-benzpyrene that, according to Gräf and Diehl (1966), range between 6.60 μg/kg of fresh matter for leeks, 12 μg/kg for lettuce and spinach and 50 μg/kg for endives.

There also seems to be at least 10 times as much of hydrocarbons in a piece of barbecued meat as in alkane yeasts; specialists believe this level could be as high as 400 μg.

Finally, according to Bories and Tulliez (private communication, 1973) the US Food and Drug Administration (FDA) has estimated that each inhabitant of the United States ingests 400 g/year of hydrocarbons and 50 g/year of mineral oils. It is true that people worry much more about what they eat than what they breathe in, or what they swallow without realizing it in saliva or through the mucus of the upper respiratory tracts.

It does not seem that the traces of aromatic polycyclic compounds found in yeasts, bacteria and algae grown on the various substrates indicated above can really be harmful. Tests carried out on domestic animals, particularly with yeasts grown on alkanes, demonstrate that, in the light of present knowledge, these products are completely innocuous.

Nevertheless, the use of yeasts grown on alkanes in foodstuffs for animals raises the question of their content in fatty acids that have an odd number of carbon atoms, and of the possibility of these acids being passed on to products of animal origin intended for human consumption. Studies carried out by various authors, including Valfré, Bosi and Belleza (1977) have shown that fatty acids with an odd number of carbon atoms can be found in the natural state in many commonly used animal foodstuffs, e.g., fish meal, oilseed cakes, cereals, cereal middlings and flakes, and fodder.

The epidermis of plants, including legumes, is covered with lipids that are rich in long-chain fatty acids, among which paraffins may predominate. The same kinds of acids are also found in the meat and fat of slaughter animals that have been reared in the traditional way, and in milk, olive oil, bread-sticks, certain fruits, etc. Detailed and accurate studies carried out by Bizzi *et al.* (1976) have shown that fatty acids with an odd number of carbon atoms are easily metabolized. These writers gave yeasts grown on alkanes to rats and found no changes in either their physiological or biological behaviour. Larger doses accounting for 80 percent of the proteins in the diet only reduced the levels of cholesterol in the adrenal glands and of triglycerides in the liver. The mobilization of lipids (from adipose tissue), cardiac function and the levels of various enzymes were not changed by eating these yeasts.

The conclusions reached by Bizzi *et al.* (1976) confirm those of other research workers. A content in fatty acids with an odd number of carbon atoms not exceeding 10 percent of the total fatty acid content of the diet (which is already a high proportion) does not seem to cause any change in normal physiological functioning. Fatty acids with an odd number of carbon atoms are, in fact, normally utilized and metabolized.

There remains the question of the level of nucleic acids in these yeasts. It has been justly objected that single-cell organisms contain a high level of nucleic acids. It is known that man's diet should contain only limited quantities of these since the purines in nucleic acid are mainly excreted in the form of uric acid. In people who are particularly sensitive to them, there may be a greater risk of gout and urinary lithiasis. It is generally agreed that the organism of an adult should not take in, via single- or multi-cell organisms, more than two grams of nucleic acids per day and that of a child even less.

There are, however, ways of lowering, in yeasts, the amount of nucleic acids which mainly derive from RNA. This can be done, for example, by growing the yeast under special conditions, combined with extraction or hydrolysis. The use of special enzymes that destroy RNA has been suggested. Use has been made, for example, of ribonuclease that is extraneous to yeasts or bacteria. Some of these methods have already been applied to strains of *Candida lipolitica* and *C. utilis* and *Bacillus subtilis*.

These processes need to be perfected before the non-traditional foods are used as food for humans. Luckily the presence of nucleic acids is not a drawback in animal foodstuffs. Except for the Dalmatian breed of dog, mammals have uricase, which oxidizes uric acid to allantoin, the final stage of the catabolism of nucleic acids. D'Mello (1973a) showed that chickens fed with yeast grown on methanol had the same level of uric acid in the blood as a control group. The same was found to be true for glutamic, oxaloacetic and pyruvic oxaloacetic transaminases of the plasma.

Some levels of nucleic acids in various yeasts are given below, although it should also be noted that the levels can vary considerably according to the growing conditions.

Organism	Nucleic acids (%)
Pseudomonas sp.	18
Candida lipolitica (60 to 80% of CPV)	9.50
Candida tropicalis (72% of CPV)	9-10
Spirulina	4.25
Ordinary dry yeast (45% of CPV)	6.00 (Birolaud, 1968)

The ratios between the level of crude protein and the level of nucleic acids in the *Candida* yeasts and in the ordinary dry yeasts are roughly the same. Much has been said about nucleic acids in new sources of single-cell protein, but little or nothing has been said about those found in traditional yeasts.

It should also be recalled that, in the thymus of calves, the nitrogen of nucleic acids represents 31 percent of the total nitrogen and that chicken embryo tissue contains 10.6 percent of these acids. According to Terroine (1960) the level of purines in meat, expressed per 100 g of fresh weight, varies from 0.14 to 0.18 g; in liver it is around 0.30 g and for fish it varies from 0.07 to 0.18 g. Finally, meat broth contains 2.5 g of purines per 100 g of broth. Champagnat and Adrian (1974) give higher figures for liver: 5.5 g/100 g of dry matter and 2.2 g/100 g of dry matter for tripe.

According to recent information (G. Durand, Institut national de la recherche agronomique [INRA], private communication), nucleic nitrogen makes up 7.75 mg/g of dry and defatted rumen bacteria, i.e., around 4.8 percent of the total nitrogen. In the muscles and liver of various animals one consistently finds the amounts indicated in Table 27.

TABLE 27. Nucleic nitrogen from DNA and RNA in tissues and foods

Animal/organism	Age/weight	Organ	Nucleic N (% of total N)	Nucleic N (mg/g of fresh tissue)
Pig	At birth	Semi-membranous muscle	4.10	0.838
	20 kg	" "	0.78	0.239
	100 kg	" "	0.45	0.160
Veal	1 month	" "	0.64	0.173
	3 months	" "	0.47	0.155
Chicken	3 weeks	Pectoral muscles	1.40	0.428
	8 weeks	" "	0.65	0.24
	12 weeks	" "	0.54	0.181
	12 weeks	Liver	5.4	1.8
Trout	20 g	Dorsal muscles	0.90	0.340
	200 g	" "	0.66	0.191
	400 g	" "	0.71	0.216
Pig	At birth	Liver	7.8	1.7
	20 kg	"	4.8	1.5
	100 kg	"	3.9	1.3
Alkane yeasts	([1])		8.7-10	6.93
	([1])		6.1	4.53

Source: M.G. Durand (INRA), personal communication.
[1] See also p. 92.

It is clear that the levels of nucleic nitrogen in yeasts are much higher than those in meat. Nevertheless, when a person eats 200 g of pork, this represents 32 mg of nucleic nitrogen; the same quantity of meat from an eight-week-old chicken would represent 48 mg. The latter quantity is about half that supplied by 10-15 g of yeast, the lysine content of which, as already noted, is equivalent to about 60 g of meat. In this case, therefore, yeasts are no longer mere additives.

As we have already seen, single- and multi-cell organisms are, on the average, quite rich in protein. The level varies between 56 and 80 percent. The balance of their constituent amino acids is also good; in particular, their richness in lysine should be noted. In Table 25 the levels of lysine (expressed for 16 g of N) goes from a minimum of 4.52 to a maximum of 10.03, i.e., always higher than the levels for soybeans and, in the case of two yeasts, higher than the levels in an egg.

It is interesting to see what percentage of the requirement of essential amino acids can be covered by some of these yeasts when used to make up 15 percent of the diet of such animals as chickens and pigs. This calculation has been done for one of the two yeasts whose use in animal feed was authorized in France at the end of 1972. The intake was compared with that given by an identical percentage of soybean cake containing 52 percent of crude protein material. Even if this reasoning is only completely valid in the case of animal feed, it does, indirectly, show the usefulness of these yeasts as supplements to cereals and, due allowance made for what was said earlier regarding nucleic acids, it can be extrapolated, *mutatis mutandis*, to man.

Data concerning the coverage of essential amino acid requirements in chickens from 0 to 4 weeks of age and for piglets weighing from 30 to 60 kg are shown in Tables 28 and 29.

Tables 28 and 29 confirm that the limiting factors for yeasts grown on alkanes are the sulphur-containing amino acids. The possibility of adding synthetic DL-methionine to the rations means that this drawback can be considered as negligible. Elmadfa and Menden (1973) observed that 0.2 percent of methionine added to yeasts (*Candida utilis*) grown on alkanes gives them a protein efficiency similar to that of casein. This has also been observed in the laboratory (see Table 30) with a supplement of 0.3 percent of methionine.

The supply of lysine is very important and, as shown earlier, 88 percent of the requirement of this amino acid is met by the yeasts, while soybeans only meet 54 percent of the requirement.

In pigs, the lysine requirement is well covered by the yeasts, while soybeans only meet 63 percent of the requirement.

In chickens, in order to ensure that the lysine requirement is fully met by soybean cake, it would be necessary (without considering the lysine content in cereals, which are low in this amino acid) to include close to 28 percent of soybean cake (considered as 52 percent of CPV [1]) in the chicken-feed ration, while only about 17 percent would be required of yeasts. Threonine is usually the third limiting factor in the diet of chickens; in this case, the

---

[1] This is an exceptionally high percentage; it is usually below 50.

TABLE 28. Extent of essential amino acid requirements met by adding yeast grown on alkanes to the feed of chickens (0 to 4 weeks old), compared with soybeans

Amino acid	Requirement [1]	Supplied by 15% yeast (72% of CPV)	Supplied by 15% soybeans (52% of CPV)	Difference between soybeans and yeasts
Arginine	1.05	0.54	0.59	− 0.05
Histidine	0.35	0.22	0.21	+ 0.01
Isoleucine	0.65	0.57	0.39	+ 0.22
Leucine	1.40	0.84	0.61	+ 0.23
Lysine	0.95	0.84	0.51	+ 0.33
Methionine + cystine	0.73	0.27	0.32	− 0.05
Phenylalanine	0.70	0.51	0.42	+ 0.09
Valine	0.85	0.62	0.42	+ 0.20
Threonine	0.70	0.58	0.31	+ 0.27
Tyrosine	0.70	0.43	0.31	+ 0.12
Tryptophan	0.20	0.14	−	−

[1] According to Calet (1968), for a ration of 2 800 kcal of metabolizable energy/kg.

TABLE 29. Extent of essential amino acid requirements met by adding yeast grown on alkanes to the feed of piglets (30 to 60 kg), compared with soybeans

Amino acid	Requirement [1]	Supplied by 15% yeast (72% of CPV)	Supplied by 15% soybeans (52% of CPV)	Difference between soybeans and yeasts
Histidine	0.21	0.22	0.21	+ 0.01
Isoleucine	0.57	0.57	0.39	+ 0.22
Leucine	0.62	0.84	0.61	+ 0.23
Lysine	0.77	0.84	0.51	+ 0.33
Methionine + cystine	0.57	0.27	0.32	− 0.05
Phenylalanine + tyrosine	0.51	0.94	0.73	+ 0.21
Valine	0.51	0.62	0.42	+ 0.20
Tryptophan	0.14	0.14	−	−

[1] According to French tables, for a ration of 0.90 FU/kg; 1 FU (fodder unit) = 2 222 kcal for pigs.

TABLE 30. Protein efficiency ratio of yeasts grown on alkanes and supplemented with 0.3 percent of DL-methionine

Item	Casein control	Yeasts					
		1	2	3	4	5	6
Protein level in the food	10.80	9.9	11.4	9.4	10.4	10.4	10.11
Number of rats in each batch	9	9	9	9	9	9	9
Mortality	0	0	0	0	1	0	0
Weight (g) Initial	45.1	45.0	45.0	45.3	45.1	44.8	44.8
Final	119.6	93.6	95.3	102.2	106.1	104.4	105.5
Gain	74.5	48.6	50.3	56.9	61	59.6	60.7
Average gain/day	2.6	1.7	1.8	2.0	2.1	2.1	2.1
Ingested protein (g)	27.8	20.5	25.9	22.4	23.8	25.3	24.1
Ingested dry matter (g)	258.1	207.6	227.6	238.4	228.9	243.6	238.2
Protein efficiency ratio	2.67	2.36	1.93	2.54	2.56	2.35	2.52
Conversion rate	3.46	4.27	4.52	4.19	3.75	4.08	3.94
Microbiological index	100	40.7	74.4	66.8	80.2	88.9	105.1

Source: Ferrando, Henry, Colonna (unpublished results, 1974).

yeasts meet 82 percent of the requirement and soybeans only 45 percent. Soybeans have a slight excess of arginine with respect to lysine, which is not found in the yeasts.

In the pig, all the dietary requirements are amply met by incorporating 15 percent of yeasts in the diet (apart from sulphur-containing amino acids, and without taking into account the cereals in the ration). A level of 13 to 14 percent of yeasts is sufficient to meet the lysine requirement, compared with 23 percent of soybean cake at 52 percent of CPV. This high content in good quality proteins (particularly lysine) of yeasts grown on alkanes should make it possible to achieve a good growth rate in pigs, with carcasses of a suitable composition, starting from a relatively low protein level (12 percent) in the diet supplemented with DL-methionine, as has been demonstrated by Rérat (1969). With 0.79 percent of lysine it is possible to achieve an average daily weight gain of 638 g and a conversion rate of 3.17.

Thus, yeasts are "utilizable" in animal feed at levels of between 12 and 17 percent, and even at lower levels of incorporation, given the other elements in the diet; and they could be used in human foodstuffs as well, despite their nucleic acids, at levels of between 10 and 20 grams/day, and perhaps even slightly higher once all or part of the nucleic acids has been removed. In view of these findings, it seems astonishing that some researchers try to test the possible toxicity of single-cell proteins by using them experimentally at the rate of 60 percent of the diet. This is a surprising approach. It has been pointed out to those who adopt it that anomalies have been found in the growth rate of rats, as well as a slight drop in their fertility, when their diet consists of 25 to 30 percent of whole-egg powder. And yet this is the control protein used. It should be noted that a diet consisting only of meat produces serious effects in the dog (Morris, Teeter and Collins, 1971). In investigations into non-traditional foods, the desire to demonstrate the absence of potential drawbacks should never be separated from the need to remain close to reality and to what is practicable.

How well are these theoretical data supported at the practical level in the light of the numerous tests that have already been carried out in several countries to determine the value, and the lack of toxicity, of single- and multi-cell organisms used in animal feed?

Quite a number of publications reporting on experiments with domestic animals have now become available. Table 31 collects some of the results obtained.

Despite the findings of Shacklady and Gatunel (1972) cited in Table 31, Japanese researchers (Tada et al., 1972) have shown that, in the laying hen, a single intake of 1 μg of vitamin B_{12} every two days, given in a diet consisting of 10 to 15 percent of yeasts grown on alkanes, improves the rate of hatching and the level of vitamin B_{12} in the eggs. In young chickens, 50 μg of vitamin B_{12} per kg of feed containing 15 percent of alkane yeasts also increases these performances (Tada et al., 1973). This is the result of a balanced diet, and such a balance cannot be ignored, even with traditional foods. This, again, is an essential point that every researcher should remember.

These results — and not all have been cited — demonstrate the value of single-cell organisms as animal feed. These products, prior to any zootechnical studies, have always been the subject of very severe toxicological tests. This subject has been studied in the publications of De Groot, Til and Feron (1971), Yoshida et al. (1972), as well as in the analytical paper of Engel (1972). Diets containing 30 percent of yeasts grown on alkanes (a percentage that, as mentioned earlier, is at the very limit of what can be tolerated) have had no harmful effects on animals receiving them throughout their life-spans. "Relay toxicity" tests have been carried out on rats

TABLE 31. Results of some tests on the food value of single- and multi-cell organisms in the feed of farm animals [1]

Animals studied	Product	Level used in the feed (%)	Results obtained	Reference
Chickens for slaughter	Yeasts grown on alkanes	7.5-15	Excellent	Shacklady and Gatumel, 1972
Laying hens, 52 weeks and three generations	Yeasts grown on alkanes	10-20	No difference from control group	Shacklady and Gatumel, 1972
Sows	Yeasts grown on alkanes	10	No harmful effect on fertility	Shacklady and Gatumel, 1972
Piglets	Yeasts grown on alkanes	7.5-15	No difference from control group	Shacklady and Gatumel, 1972
Calves	Yeasts grown on alkanes	20-50	Very good	Shacklady and Gatumel, 1972
Calves	Yeasts grown on alkanes	70-75% of CPV	Very good	Paruelle et al., 1972
Chickens	Yeasts on methanol	4.9-9.8	No difference from control group	ICI records
Pigs and piglets	Yeasts on methanol	2.5-14	No difference from control group	ICI records
Laying hens, first generation	Yeasts on alkanes	15	No difference from control group	Yoshida et al., 1972
Laying hens, second and third generations	Yeasts on alkanes	15	No difference from control group	Yoshida et al., 1973

TABLE 31. Results of some tests on the food value of single- and multi-cell organisms in the feed of farm animals [1] *(concluded)*

Animals studied	Product	Level used in the feed (%)	Results obtained	Reference
Chickens	Yeasts on methanol	4.9-9.8	No difference from control group	D'Mello, 1973a
Chickens	Yeasts on alkanes	15	Good	D'Mello, 1973a
Chickens	Yeasts on alkanes	22.75	Drop in growth rate	D'Mello, 1973a
Pigs	Yeasts on alkanes	6.4	Good	Yarov, Basargin and Shcherbak, 1973
Pigs	Yeasts on alkanes	From 6 to 250 g/day	Good	Garkavaya and Ramanis, 1971a,b
Pigs	Yeasts on alkanes	10-16	Good	Kneale, 1972
Pigs	Yeasts on alkanes	7.6	Good	Garkavaya and Ramanis, 1971b
Pigs and piglets	Yeasts on alkanes	7.5-15	Good	Van der Wal *et al.*, 1971
Sows	Yeasts on alkanes	28	No harmful effect on metabolism or fertility	Nozdrin, 1969
Boars	Yeasts on alkanes	20	No harmful effect on metabolism or fertility	Doktorovich, 1969
Carp	Yeasts on alkanes	30	Good	Oomae, 1971

[1] These are preliminary results. The official and unofficial results that have been published since 1973 confirm those shown in the table.

using the meat, liver, kidneys and fat of pigs and chickens that had been fed on rations containing such yeasts and no harmful effects were observed. Finally, various checks have shown that the organoleptic qualities of products obtained from farm animals thus fed are normal.

However, it seems that the mere use of a non-traditional substrate is enough to arouse suspicion. The fact that there has been so much talk of "protein from petrol" or "steaks from oil" has not helped. When it comes to food it is best to avoid the unusual. There are certain words that may be very eye-catching immediately but that are dangerous in the long term, since they carry overtones that make people uneasy. Even the most extreme revolutionary is a strict conservative when it comes to matters of food.

As regards food for humans, no large-scale tests have yet been carried out with single-cell or multi-cell organisms, except in the case of *Spirulina*, which was tested at the level of 2 percent in the diets of volunteers in Mexico and France. The amount of *Spirulina* given to French consumers who agreed to eat this seaweed was either 1/7 or 1/4 of the total protein nitrogen. The results appeared to be similar to those obtained with the control diets. Nevertheless, although acceptance was good in Mexico for foods containing 2 percent of *Spirulina*, it was not so good in France. Depigmentation of the product does not remove its disagreeable taste. Further studies are therefore needed. Mueller-Wecker and Kofranyt (1973) demonstrated by means of tests carried out on six young men that the eating of the alga *Scenedesmus obliquus* improves the protein efficiency of the diet without any increase in the level of uric acid in the blood. They consider as allowable an addition to the diet of 20 to 30 g/day. However, *Saccharomyces cerevisiae* is less usable. This yeast has only a slight effect on the efficiency of the diet and causes an increase in blood uric acid level. An intake of 10 g/day per subject should not be exceeded.

Properly tested single-cell or multi-cell organisms do not appear to constitute a danger for animals, nor, it would seem, for humans, although there will have to be further studies in order to make these new food sources more attractive to the human consumer. What happened with them in Japan is instructive although there it was only a question of feed for stock animals.

However, the substitution in stock farming of these proteins [1] for the powdered milk used in feed for suckling animals should soon make larger quantities of powdered milk available for food aid to the Third World. At FAO's 17th Conference in November 1973, P. Lardinois stressed the need to use increasing amounts of milk products in these countries, as was done in India during the project known as "Operation Flood".

---

[1] The subsequent rise in the price of crude oil has altered these aspects of the problem.

From the purely nutritional point of view, these single-cell and multi-cell organisms are high-quality proteins. Their nucleic acid content does not affect animals. Nevertheless, any new product of this type must be fully tested before its use can be authorized. It is essential to check that its composition remains constant and, of course, that no harmful substances are present. This constancy, especially of amino acid composition, is one of the principal qualities of single-cell and multi-cell organisms and it is important to preserve it as much as possible.

Industrial processing of non-traditional foods

Over and above any question relating to protein requirements, the non-traditional food sources that have been examined can, after mixing with small quantities of nutritive elements that are recognized as being essential to man, constitute a complete food, the appearance, texture and taste of which can be infinitely varied. Already there are vegetable creams and protein-enriched drinks resembling fruit juices. There is also, for example, a drink enriched with fungi hydrolysed according to a patent of Mori and Miyashita (1974), and artificial cheeses that certainly do not contain any amines. In this area almost anything is possible. The economic goal is to "short-circuit" the animal stage without disturbing the consumer either physiologically or psychologically, while, at the same time, saving energy.

To reach this goal, three important problems have to be solved concerning:

● *Protein balance.* The composition of these new foods should be, as far as possible, identical or at least very close to that of protein of animal origin.
● *Appearance.* It is worth making the effort to overcome consumer resistance. No one has ever eaten − much less paid money for − a product solely on account of its amino-acid, trace mineral element or vitamin content.
● *Cost.* This will have to be better than competitive with traditional foods so that consumers, who are normally more conservative in matters of gastronomy than in any other field, will change their eating habits. The production of yeasts on alkanes was abandoned in some countries as the price of crude oil went up and that for soybeans went down.

To achieve these aims, research has been going on for a long time in order to perfect the transformation of proteins of diverse origins (particularly vegetable) into proteins that can be eaten by man. The choice has been between cereals, oilseed cakes, leguminous seeds, green plants (leaf protein) and, finally, the various categories of single-cell or multi-cell organisms. A general review of this question has been carried out by Bombal *et al.* (1974), to which we shall be making frequent reference here.

Long before US industrialists became interested in the problem, small-scale processes, at the artisan level, had been employed in the Far East to manufacture foods from the soybean. Around 1930, when this plant began to be grown in the USA, the food-processing companies started to market products similar to those produced by small-scale methods in Asia. The best known was a drink, soybean milk, which joined soybean oil on the table of the US consumer (Kingsbaker, 1970). An effort was thus already being made to exploit soybeans as human food for their high protein and oil content. The idea of the protein value of soybeans was to be developed alongside the oil-content value.

These soybean products found a ready market among the Asian population living on the West Coast of the USA and among the members of various vegetarian, religious sects. Nevertheless, this market represented only a tiny percentage of the tonnage of soybeans processed.

Among proteins of vegetable origin, those obtained from various seeds such as soybeans, groundnuts, and cotton currently lend themselves best to processing for the following reasons:

Large quantities of these seeds are available at a relatively low cost, which is determined by that of the raw vegetable material and its protein content (taking into account the value of the oil which, unlike before, is increasingly being considered as a by-product). The high protein content avoids the need for costly and complicated technology to bring the percentage of proteins up to the levels found in meat. The amounts of protein that can be extracted from the seeds (see Table 32) are, at least at the moment and certainly in the case of three or four of them, superior to those obtained from green plants and, possibly, are more easily extracted. However, it is true that the CPV level in certain leaf-protein concentrates can reach 60 percent.

Furthermore, the raw materials used, e.g., seeds (and especially seed-cakes), have a suitable amino-acid balance in their protein (see Table 33). We are still, however, a long way from the balance found in leaf proteins and single-cell or multi-cell organisms, although the problems to be solved regarding toxicity and production techniques seem, at first sight, less important.

Actually, many of these raw materials can still contain toxic substances. Some cause minor effects on the organism and are capable of being easily eliminated. Others are dangerous toxins. Soybeans belong to the first group, while groundnuts and cottonseed belong to the second because of the aflatoxins and mycotoxins found in both and the gossypol that is present in

TABLE 32. Protein matter in different oilcakes (N × 6.25)
(Percentage)

Cake	Protein content
Soybean	43.0-51
Groundnut	41.0-50
Linseed	30.0-37
Sunflower	[1] 19.6-55
Cottonseed	[1] 28.0-45
Rapeseed	30.0-37
Copra	20.0-24
Palm oil	15.0-19

Source: Ferrando (1972b).
[1] Depending on whether the seed has been shelled or not.

TABLE 33. Comparative levels of essential amino acids in different sources of protein

Amino acid	Pressed soybean cake	Soybean protein concentrate	Ground-nut cake	Rapeseed cake	Calf muscle	Whole hen's egg
Arginine	7.3	8.3	10.4	6.0	6.8	6.6
Histidine	2.4	2.6	2.9	2.7	2.4	2.4
Isoleucine	5.3	6.5	3.3	4.2	5.5	6.8
Leucine	7.7	6.8	6.4	6.8	8.7	9.0
Lysine	6.3	6.8	3.3	5.3	9.4	6.3
Methionine	1.4	1.0	0.8	2.0	2.8	3.1
Cystine	1.6	–	1.2	2.7	1.3	2.3
Phenylalanine	4.9	5.0	5.1	4.1	4.5	5.9
Threonine	3.9	3.9	2.6	4.4	4.8	5.0
Valine	5.2	5.5	3.7	5.5	6.3	7.4
Tryptophan	1.4	1.0	0.9	–	–	1.7
Tyrosine	3.2	3.4	4.1	3.3	3.7	4.4

Source: Lefebvre (1970).

cottonseed. Rape, which is less rich in proteins, has to be totally freed of its antithyroid compounds before it can be used in the preparation of non-traditional foods. It has already been shown (page 68) that various processes exist to do this. In short, only proteins derived from soybeans are currently used for the preparation of non-traditional foods. In the future other sources of protein will be used as well, particularly the seeds already mentioned as well as kidney beans, field beans and other beans, leaf protein and, finally, protein from single-cell or multi-cell organisms grown on various substrates, particularly alkanes.

The various methods of processing soybeans, which will now be discussed in connection with the manufacture of non-traditional foods, can be applied, with some slight modifications, to other agricultural protein sources.

It should be possible to use single-cell and multi-cell organisms directly in the manufacture of new foods and to enrich biscuits, pasta, semolina, or in the preparation of hydrolysates.

The processing of seeds and cakes made from them is mainly concerned with concentrating proteins and altering their structure. The processes of husking and flaking the seeds (see Figure 1) are now well developed for soybeans (Wilding, 1970).

There is a problem, however, in removing the last traces of solvent from the defatted flakes that are used to prepare non-traditional foods. There are various processes adapted to produce specific types of flour, i.e., to the protein levels required.

The wet flakes, containing up to 30 percent of hexane, pass through very hot air, which quickly evaporates any traces of solvent still remaining in the flakes.

The flakes then go through a deodorizing machine (for "toasting"), which operates under a partial vacuum so that the steam does not condense (Horan, 1967). The proteins are not denatured during these operations, except for a slight denaturing during toasting.

Three classic types of flour are obtained: flours defatted to 50 percent of proteins; "low fat" flours, at 46 percent; "full fat" flour at 41 percent (Kingsbaker, 1970).

For industrial purposes, one can use: defatted flours containing around 50 percent of CPV; concentrated flours with 70 percent of CPV; proteins isolated from soybeans at 97 percent of CPV (Aspinall, 1967) (see Figure 1). In preparing the concentrated flours and the proteins isolated from soybeans the soluble carbohydrates are eliminated. The isolated proteins are used mainly for their technological properties.

The development of textured proteins from soybeans is encouraged by the fact that technology makes it possible to transform a product still in a

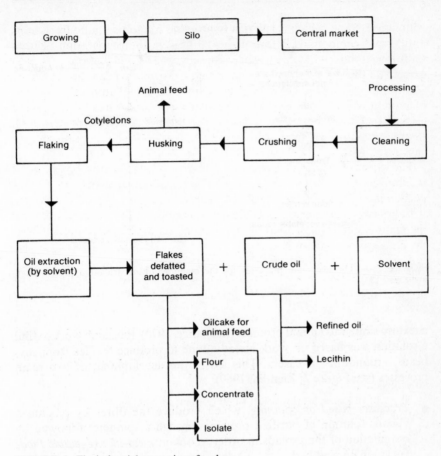

FIGURE 1. The industrial processing of soybeans

crude state, the cost price of which remains competitive with that of other protein sources (Wolf and Cowan, 1971).

How are these "textured" proteins prepared?

While the protein-bearing fibres of muscle or support tissue consist of bundles made of lengthened and oriented polypeptide chains, soybean proteins are globular proteins, which in solution are in the form of isolated molecules or in a small number of associations of sub-units.

Muscle proteins are not soluble in water while those from soybeans are, except near their isoelectric point (pH 4.5).

The problems are to transform these globular, water-soluble proteins into proteins with a fibrous structure that are not water-soluble, and to give them

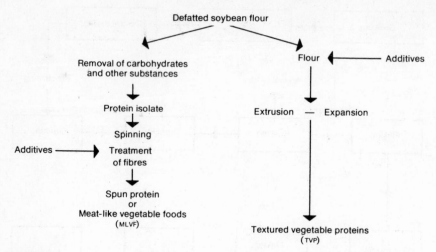

FIGURE 2. – The two main processes for the manufacture of structured protein from soybeans

a texture similar to animal proteins (Lachance, 1970). Research work to find a solution was based on work already done to produce textiles from soybeans, groundnuts or casein. This led to the development of two main processes (see Figure 2; Ziemba, 1969):

● *Processes based on spinning*, which produce the fibres by passing a viscous solution of purified proteins through a spinneret followed by coagulation of the threads in order to obtain *meat-like vegetable foods* (MLVF) in an acid bath;
● *The extrusion processes*, in which the protein mixture is heat-treated before being extruded to produce textured vegetable protein (TVP; Lefebvre, 1970).

There are several patents for spun protein which differ only slightly in their general principle, including those of Boyer (1954, 1959), Boyer and Saewert (1956) and Westeen and Kuramoto (1964). The latter were engineers in the automotive industry.

Figure 3 (the process patented by Westeen and Kuramoto) shows the protein-extraction and purification operations and the subsequent formation of a viscous protein solution from which are formed fibres with diameters of between 0.5 and 1.5 mm. During this treatment the polypeptide chains (the globular structure of which has previously been destroyed)

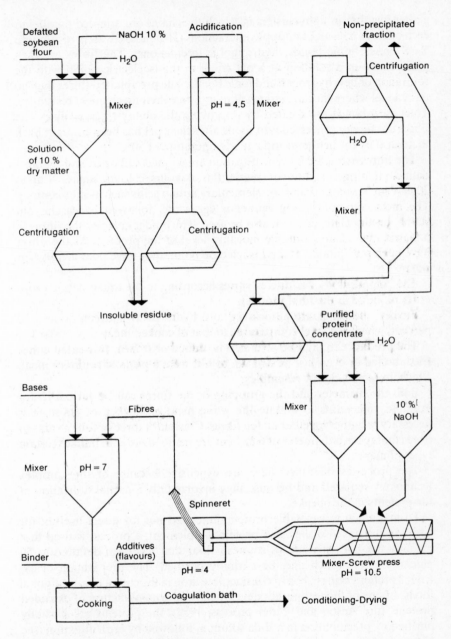

FIGURE 3. The Westeen and Kuramoto process

gather together in tight clusters in which the chains are oriented parallel to each other as a result of multiple interactions (H-bonds; covalent disulphide S-S bonds; ionic bonds; hydrophobic interactions). The fibres are then precipitated in a solution at a pH equal to the isoelectric point, with the formation of new hydrogen and ionic bonds. The precipitated fibres then go onto a reel where they are stretched to improve their mechanical resistance. Thus, new bonds are created by improving the ability to crystallize. The fibres are finally processed into foods after their pH has been brought back to neutral by the action of soda at a temperature of 30°C.

The fibres extracted by centrifugation are washed and dried and sent to a bath containing the additives (binder fats, flavours, colours, sugars − up to 20 percent − vitamins and supplementary amino acids such as methionine). The most commonly used binder is egg-white, followed by casein, but starch, pectin, algin, etc., can also be used. The binder encloses the fibres in a matrix and ensures suitable moisture level of the product. As the fibres have been precipitated at their isoelectric point, they have poor affinity for water.

The composition of additives varies according to the organoleptic properties required in the final product.

Finally, the fibres are autoclaved and hydrated to between 50 and 70 percent, which is a level comparable to that of cooked meat.

The product can then be sold as it is, tinned or frozen. It is eaten either fried, boiled or even just heated up, as if it were a piece of ordinary meat, which, in fact, it closely resembles.

Both the diameter and the grouping of the fibres can be varied. If, for example, one wants to imitate the white meat of chicken or goose, it is necessary to gather together all the fibres. Clusters of three or four groups of fibres that reach a diameter of 6 to 7 cm are made in order to imitate certain types of meat.

The processes described here are expensive because of the complex technology required and because they involve only a partial utilization of the proteins in the oilcake.

To manufacture vegetable proteins intended not for direct use but for addition to cooked dishes as a protein supplement, a process is used that involves the hot extrusion of soybean flour that has been defatted to 50 percent of CPV, which may be partially purified. The preparation of extruded proteins brings about a considerable drop in the cost of non-traditional foods. In one of the techniques developed for the manufacture of extruded proteins (the Anson and Pader process, 1959), the proteins are partially purified by precipitation in a soda solution, followed by centrifugation (see Figure 4). After bringing the solution back to its isoelectric point one obtains a gel used as a precursor. This is sent to the extruder together with a soda

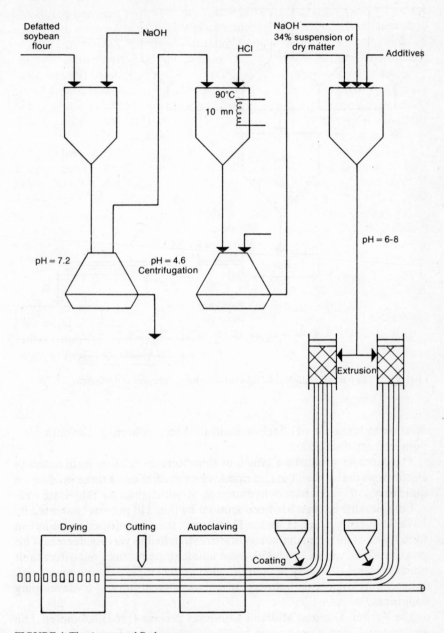

FIGURE 4. The Anson and Pader process

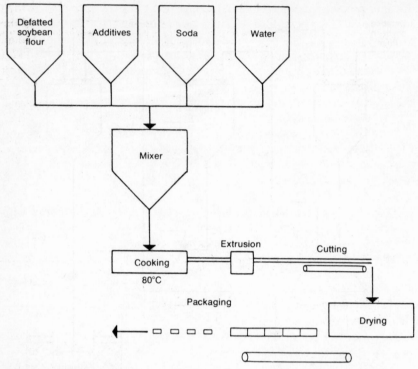

FIGURE 5. The Archer, Daniels, Midland process (from Crémiers and Maubras, 1972)

solution to bring the pH back to neutral. Water, colouring, flavours, vitamins, etc. are then added.

The extruder produces a tangle of thin "vermicelli" that form a sort of elastic mass that is then cut and dried. The rehydration of these products is quite easy, compared with dehydrated meat, which does not rehydrate well.

Considerable interest has been aroused by the "Hd process" patented by Laval University, Canada. In the Hd process, the non-purified proteins can form fibres of different diameters that are stretched to varying degrees. This process, which can be used with most edible proteins, does not affect their nutritive value. It is easy to operate and can be employed both on a small scale and in large-scale industry. It is thus of great interest to developing countries.

The Archer, Daniels, Midland Company process (1967) is simpler. The raw material used is once again soybean flour that has been defatted to 50 percent of CPV. It is then mixed with water, soda and other additives and the alkaline protein solution forms a homogeneous plastic mass that is then heated to 80°C and extruded at low temperature and low pressure in the presence of an inert gas. This makes the water contained in the product boil, causing it to expand (Figure 5). The Reinhart and Sair process (1971, 1973) is similar to the Archer process. The Wenger process is currently the most widely used.

This is the process used in the manufacture of the textured vegetable protein now sold in France[1].

Apart from cost (the cost ratio is around 1 to 30-40 for beef and pork and 1 to 10-12 for chicken meat), the non-traditional foods made from textured protein have other advantages.

TABLE 34. Amino acids in textured vegetable proteins, compared with meat
(Expressed as g per 100 g of product)

Amino acid	Textured food		Cooked beef
	Spun protein	Extruded protein	
Tryptophan	0.46	0.27	0.23
Isoleucine	1.04	1.07	1.02
Leucine	1.79	1.54	1.60
Threonine	0.94	0.77	0.86
Lysine	1.41	1.20	1.70
Methionine	0.36	0.22	0.48
Cystine	0.71	0.28	0.25
Phenylalanine	1.29	1.09	0.80
Tyrosine	0.84	0.79	0.66
Valine	1.22	1.17	1.08

After adding synthetic methionine and lysine (Kies and Fox, 1971), the soybean protein and spun proteins sold on the market have a level of amino acids that is higher than, or identical to, that of cooked meat. Table 34 shows the levels of essential amino acids in these products, compared with cooked beef.

---

[1] There is a pilot plant at Vénissieux, near Lyon.

TABLE 35. Protein efficiency ratio and biological value of various textured protein foods and traditional protein foods

Food	Protein efficiency ratio	Biological value
Spun proteins	2.3-2.4	80
Extruded proteins	1.8-2.0	75-81
Casein	2.5	
Beef	3.2	76
Egg (reference)	3.8	94
Wheat	1.5	0

Source: Gubler (1968).

The protein efficiency ratio and the biological value of these products compare well with other traditional foods, according to Thulin and Kuramoto (1967) as well as other authors (see Table 35).

The protein value of these various foods will finally reflect that of soybean oilcake, provided that technological treatments have not destroyed too high a percentage of amino acids. Thus, spun proteins, which do not undergo violent heat treatment, have a protein value higher than that of extruded proteins, which are, in part, denatured by cooking (Martin, 1970).

It should be recalled that the nutritive value of these foods can be improved by the addition of methionine. In this way one obtains an increase of more than 20 percent in protein efficiency ratio. But, in practice, this is not done, since these products are only used to complement other sources of proteins. It is quite conceivable, however, that without using synthetic methionine, one could provide a methionine supplement by using protein binders from sunflower or sesame seeds, which, although they are poor in lysine, are rich in methionine. There is every possibility of supplying these foods with all the essential substances required for good nutrition, including essential fatty acids, calcium, magnesium, trace mineral elements or vitamins. It would thus be possible to provide, in a palatable form, a food that is truly complete, totally harmless and perfectly adapted to a given physiological, or even pathological, situation. It should also be stressed that for products of vegetable origin, the cellulose content is low. It is always less than 3 percent of dry matter, and can be even lower, as in spun proteins.

The trypsin inhibitors in soybeans are completely destroyed during technological processing, which also removes the disagreeable taste of the soybeans; the taste can also be masked by certain flavourings.

Some authors, such as Althoff (1970), have observed that structured proteins can produce flatulence as a result of the presence of indigestible carbohydrates, such as raffinose and stachyose, which were mentioned earlier. There exist, however, natural antiflatulent compounds, which could be used as they are quite easy to synthesize.

The papers of Gounelle de Pontanel and Dumas-Astier (1970) and, more recently, of Poullain, Guisard and Debry (1972) show, in 10 nitrogen-balance studies carried out on man, that these products are quite acceptable. The consumer's metabolism is not upset. Other trials have shown that these proteins are very easily digested.

The bacteriological characteristics of these foods are far superior to those of meat products in general. Their germ-count is less than 500 per gram [1].

Nevertheless, the need to examine carefully the harmlessness of these new products before they can be put on the market must be stressed. The processing of the various proteins used may not only alter their food value but can cause them to have varying degrees of toxicity. It is known, for example, that one of the soybean proteins, the α-protein, can cause changes to the proximal part of the kidney tubules. A thermostable nephrotoxic factor seems to be induced (Woodard and Short, 1973) by treatment with 0.1 N soda during the preparation of this α-protein. It seems to be a toxic derivative of lysine called lysinoalanine. This matter was taken up again by Sternberg, Kim and Schwende (1975) who refer to the work cited. Mention should also be made of the work done by De Groot and Shump (in 1969 and, with Feron and Van Beek, in 1976). Treatment with bases to extract proteins may also cause destruction of methionine, serine, threonine and arginine [2].

Consequently, it is worth while establishing procedures for the study of any possible toxicity in each new non-traditional food as well as techniques that will allow them to be identified in the general framework of food control.

This knowledge will determine the possibility of adding these products to human food.

The length and effect of storage should also be studied. These can be limiting factors to the consumption of some non-traditional foods just as

---

[1] Bacteriological tests carried out on yeasts grown on alkanes have also shown that their quality is excellent. Their germ-count is well below that of fish meals or meat currently being sold on the market.

[2] Lysinoalanine is found in traditional foods (casein, frankfurters, etc.). Moreover, the rat seems very sensitive to this amino acid (Sternberg, Kim and Schwende, 1975). Van Stratum et al. (1978) showed that these new proteins from soybeans can replace 25 percent of the traditional proteins in man without any untoward effects.

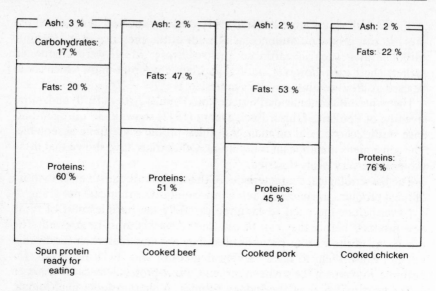

FIGURE 6. Composition of spun protein and cooked meats (the content of the former is actually lower)

they can be for traditional foods. Spun protein cannot be stored for much longer than six weeks because the added fats become rancid. However, the possibility could be considered of adding antioxidants that are permitted in foods, such as butylated hydroxyanisole (BHA) and butylated hydroxytoluene (BHT), or even certain tocopherols. As regards textured proteins, there is no apparent change even after they have been preserved for several years.

The presentation and use of these non-traditional foods based on spun or extruded proteins will now be considered.

Spun proteins are very similar to meat both in physical structure and in organoleptic qualities; hence the name "meat-like vegetable foods" (MLVF) and their sale as a substitute for meat to be consumed as sold (Rakosky, 1970).

These foods contain a high percentage of protein-rich fibres and generally have the appearance of granules: small pieces measuring between 0.5 and 3 cm in diameter, or, as larger pieces with a diameter of 6 to 7 cm that look like *filet mignon*. Such foods have to be rehydrated before being used by heating in hot water, which increases their water content from 6 to 50-70 percent, i.e., to a level comparable with that in cooked meat. In order to reach a wider market, some of these products can be presented directly in rehydrated slices, as is done with pieces of ordinary meat, and then cooked as such (Thulin and Kuramoto, 1967).

TABLE 36. Composition of an expanded, extruded seedcake

Composition	Hydrated, expanded, extruded seedcake	Medium-fat raw beef
Water	70.0	60.0
Proteins	16.3	17.0
Fats	0.3	20.0
Carbohydrates	11.4	0.5
Ash	2.0	2.5

Source: Archer, Daniels, Midland Company (1967).

The composition of products based on spun protein is very close to that of most meats and usually differs only by having a lower fat and higher carbohydrate content, as shown in Figure 6 (Thulin and Kuramoto, 1967).

As a meat substitute, spun proteins have a rather special and not very widespread market.

Extruded proteins are not aimed at the same consumer that spun proteins are aimed at. They are not only sold as meat substitutes but also as a protein supplement to food based on meat. Expanded, extruded products or textured vegetable proteins (TVP) are presented under the form of small flakes or granules about the size of a small nut. When rehydrated prior to consumption they absorb about double their weight of water. Their composition is then little different from that of average-quality beef (see Table 36).

Extruded products contain less protein than the spun product – 50 percent as opposed to 70 percent – and contain the original soybean carbohydrates. These non-traditional foods represent 95 percent of the US market for soybean-based textured proteins thanks to the fact that their price is much lower than that of spun proteins.

Thus, soybean flour is currently used as a protein source in various sectors of the food industry: in cakes, ice cream, baby food and "junior" foods, dietetic foods, etc. (Burket, 1971). According to Wilding (1970), nearly 19 million kg of soybean flour and semolina were used to prepare meat-like products. According to Kreh (1970) US consumers are suspicious of these new foods, but opinion has since changed, particularly because of the low fat content of these products. According to statistics for 1976, production of these products is now somewhere between 300 000 and 350 000 tons per year, of which some 6 500 tons are exported to Europe where the market is still limited. The clandestine use that is made of these products, particularly in market tests, makes it difficult to arrive at a good estimate. Specialists are of the opinion that in a country like France the sale of vegetable protein will only represent 2 percent of the protein intake by 1985-88 [1]. It should also be remembered that the consumer lumps every new source of protein together with other proteins, such as those of yeasts grown on alkanes, which are the very symbol of a futuristic artificial food and which are praised and rejected at the same time, tainted with the absurd name of "petrol proteins". Only "snack" foods seem to escape from this prejudice and the manufacturers of spun protein hope to capture a portion of this market, which, according to Hamdy (1968), is worth around four thousand million US dollars.

However, textured proteins have a much wider outlet in the field of catering for large groups, school and factory canteens, hospitals, etc. The use of non-traditional foods results in economies that allow for meals to be improved by means of an extra intake of yoghurts or milk side-dishes (Contour and Gubler, 1972), while helping to provide balanced meals and the preparation of dietetic foods for low-calorie and low-fat diets, as well as of food for young children, i.e., the "junior" foods mentioned earlier.

The meat-processing industry, for its part, can use large quantities of textured vegetable protein to replace some of its need for lean meat, while still preserving the basic organoleptic qualities of the particular preparation. After rehydration these products can be frozen, cut or ground just like meat. They are used in hamburgers, pies, stuffing, ravioli, various prepared dishes, etc. The market for structured proteins seems wider than that for spun protein, because the main restraints on their consumption disappear: the consumer's habits are not upset and the organoleptic qualities of the prepared products are preserved. Nevertheless, as soon as the consumer suspects that a product contains even a slight percentage of soybean protein he or she has a definite tendency to cut back on its purchase. What will happen when the consumer suspects the presence of proteins extracted from rape or single-cell or multi-cell organisms?

In catering for large groups, however, the situation is different and the use of non-traditional foods can continue to spread even if cooks sometimes refuse to use them. The obligation to inform the consumer as to the addition of such foods to certain meat dishes makes many catering companies and organizations hesitate to use them, owing to the poor image these substances have [2].

---

[1] *Le marché mondial du soja.* Paris, Caisse centrale de coopération économique, 1978.

[2] However, one should not forget the possibilities in the pet foods market.

Although regulations on the use of these products are now being drawn up, the US Department of Agriculture has already recommended (in USDA Report No.·219) their use in association with meat for school canteens, provided that the percentage of rehydrated product (60 to 65 percent water) does not exceed 30 percent of the total in the dish, as eaten.

Although, in theory, there seems to be a clear interest in using structured proteins, in practice, the hopes of the manufacturers of non-traditional foods have not been fulfilled. The sale of these non-traditional foods has mostly developed in the United States (1 800 tons in 1971). The big food-processing companies invested heavily in this sector, after being encouraged by a promising initial take-off (US$10 million in 1969), and by the forecasts of the Department of Agriculture, which estimated that, in 1980, the development of vegetable textured protein would involve about 5 percent of the US market for meat, i.e., the equivalent of 1 800 000 tons, of which 4 to 8 percent is chicken meat. At a more general level, according to the projections of Hammonds and Call (1970), over two thousand million pounds weight of product (dry matter basis) derived from soybeans will be used in human food in 1980.

In Europe, according to Contour (1970), the only countries with significant sales were the UK, Sweden and France. At the time of writing (1977) they total 20 000 tons, 15 000 tons of which refer to the UK. The French company that sells the product seems only moderately optimistic for the future. Even though one can count on publicity and an evolution in consumer taste to make a place for these products in the human diet, there will still be many difficulties. In spite of what several industrial groups wish, one cannot, and must not, make a distinction between food for the masses and food for an élite. Only an evolution in life styles, if it were to continue, could change eating habits completely. This evolution is bound up with urbanization, which, hopefully, cannot continue at its present excessive rate. The theoretical view has been clearly defined by Dahan (1973): he wrote that innovations in the matter of food products merit much more care than has been given to them in the past and that there have been relatively few major developments in the sector of new foods (excluding the discovery of deep-freezing and freeze-drying). Dahan was referring to France. Elsewhere, the effort to introduce new foods is more varied but it still comes up against the conservative instincts of the consumer.

Contrary to expectations, it has not been in the countries of the Third World, which are frequently tragically lacking in quality proteins, that textured proteins have found an outlet, but rather in the industrialized countries whose protein deficit is, in reality, a luxury deficit since the inhabitants of these countries have the highest meat intake per caput. This paradoxical situation can, however, be explained, in terms of money. How can the developing countries afford to buy these non-traditional foods, which may seem cheap to people living in a post-industrial civilization but are still too expensive for most people in other countries?

Before introducing the use of these non-traditional foods on a large scale in the countries of the Third World, it is equally important to have them accepted by the countries of Europe and North America. The fact that these foodstuffs account for such a small part of the meat market, or the market in general, shows, as mentioned earlier, that there is still a long way to go.

It should be fully realized that, as regards food and eating, the myth of the natural food is still solidly rooted in the minds of men, whether they live in industrialized or developing countries. Why should one person be willing to eat foods that another hesitates over? Everywhere, traditions regarding nutrition have been formed by a mixture of habit, false science and religious taboos and beliefs, and these traditions are solidly entrenched, even among highly educated people in industrialized countries. The Japanese experience is a case in point, when the question arose of using proteins from yeast grown on alkanes simply to feed animals. Of course, Minamata disease and itai-itai disease have made the inhabitants of that country particularly sensitive.

Without going so far as to use proteins from single-cell or multi-cell organisms immediately, a restructuring of agriculture should enable us to increase our protein resources. Von Pufendorf (1974) has rightly stressed the scant interest regarding agriculture shown by economic policy-makers. He points out that it is essential to promote new technologies that will increase the demand for labour and produce a better coordination between the various aspects of agricultural, industrial, regional and structural policies that would give priority to the problem of employment. He goes on to say that we must rediscover agriculture and the agricultural and food-processing industries and accept the need completely to reconsider the concept of expansion at all costs, based on an industrialization that neglects agriculture or directs it into channels dangerous for the environment, as well as the fact that the constraints imposed on agriculture to adapt to general growth rates only increase the instability of ecological systems, the limits of which then become only too evident. Systems of agricultural and food-processing industries should be devised in such a way that they are tailored to man, i.e., they should be regional, not multinational. The production techniques available for non-traditional foods and, of course, for traditional foods should make it possible to achieve this harmoniously, i.e., by respecting the best conditions of a biology applied to man and his welfare. It is not at all certain that excessive urbanization and industrialization form part of this biology. They are, rather, more likely to be its negation.

This evolution should be accompanied by a programme to disseminate information and knowledge regarding eating habits, and traditional and non-traditional foods. Nutrition and its application to diets are not at all a familiar topic. It is surprising how a topic that is so fundamental to health, at the very basis of life, should be so ignored and play such a relatively small role in our societies. An effort should be made, therefore, to get politicians to recognize this need and to think more about agriculture and food matters.

Finally, current legislation should be adapted to the evolution of nutrition science and techniques related to it, at least as regards the preparation of non-traditional foods and the need for better knowledge of traditional foods. This will be the subject of the final section of this book. Current activities in this sector will be described as well as facts that, if they were better known by the public at large, could calm its anxiety while making it face up to the realities of an era where cultivable land is diminishing at a worrisome rate.

Part Three

PROTECTING THE CONSUMER

INTERNATIONAL ACTIVITIES FOR CONSUMER PROTECTION

Introduction

When one looks at what has been written about traditional and non-traditional foods, it is clear that it is the idea of quality that predominates; however, this notion is never evaluated in the same way for both types of food.

The consumer undoubtedly prefers traditional foods, provided they are "natural". The difficulty, not to say the impossibility, of defining this concept has been discussed. Nature can, depending on circumstances, give man natural things that are to some degree harmful. Even before man had found the means to combat crop damage caused by insects and moulds, the plants themselves, as has already been shown, were producing substances capable of preventing, or at least reducing the damage. These same substances often have effects on the consumer that can be harmful to varying degrees.

Thus a biological equilibrium was established that was quite acceptable for a set of circumstances that, in other times, regulated a weighted demographic growth within the social structures, balancing rural and urban populations. In short, it was as if the plants had their own natural pesticides that were sufficient to ensure a minumum of protection for reasonable conditions of growth. When these conditions were exceeded or disturbed it was necessary to find something else, not only to protect the plants and animals, but to increase production. Failure to do so meant that populations that were too numerous or too concentrated ran the risk (as they still do) of starvation and even death.

From that moment on, the notion of quality in traditional food has been doubly disturbed, first of all by nature's own mechanisms and then by man's intervention. The consumer knows nothing of the first and has mixed views about the second. Finally, when it comes to non-traditional foods, this preoccupation takes on even larger dimensions. The notion of quality remains rather vague for him but it is still closely linked to the (equally vague) concept that he has, or thinks he has, of what "natural" means.

However, quality is a concept that varies greatly when one moves away from the dictates of health. Even within the framework of health requirements, the quality of a meal to be eaten by a healthy man will be very different from the meal recommended for a diabetic or obese person. Sometimes, even, as a result of economic necessity or the particular requirements of the consumer, what is considered quality can be in conflict with safety considerations laid down by a health specialist. Quality is a very relative concept in the market-place. In the end it comes down to the needs and requirements of the consumers who, as we have already seen, are not always the best judges of quality; in any case, the physiological state or the health of the consumer can alter his needs without him being aware of it.

Quality may be developed, changed, adapted or decreased, but it is always checked all along the food chain. The plant and the animal are always relays, transforming balances present in the crop and ration to the quality of the product and thus to the foodstuff required by the consumer, who may even require a quality that involves a nutritional imbalance in the animal feed. In this connection it should be noted that a lack of quality, seen in the absolute terms of nutritional balance, is sometimes actually a result of the preparation of a rare or sought-after quality, even though from the biological standpoint it is a faulty quality. *Foie gras* is a case in point. Quality food or quality feeding is that which is able to meet the normal or distorted needs of an animal in the most economical way (even if its health is affected), in order to produce foods that are the most acceptable to, or the most sought after by, the consumer. This should be done without affecting his health by means of harmful residues, but not necessarily producing a food of animal or vegetable origin that is perfectly balanced from the nutritional standpoint.

Conversely, it is possible to produce foods that are better adapted to meet certain requirements of the consumer or of a particular group of consumers. There are a number of ways of satisfying the requirements of human dietetics through a more sophisticated and planned method of animal feeding or, more simply, through modifications of the animal's diet so that it will bypass or deceive some of the animal's normal metabolic processes.

Techniques exist to produce meat, eggs and milk with higher levels of essential fatty acids, particularly linoleic acid. It is well known that this acid plays a role in the prevention of cardiovascular disease and in the biological synthesis of prostaglandins.

There is also the possibility of preparing non-traditional foods that are adapted perfectly to the needs of the consumer in so far as our present knowledge of nutrition requirements allows us to define such needs. The same is true of the microorganisms used in industry. By means of genetic manipulation or by using special culture conditions metabolic products that are of nutritional interest can be accumulated: amino acids, vitamins, antibiotics, steroids. In this way it has been possible to prepare lysine by fermentation. In agriculture, the new strains of maize, 'Opaque-2' and 'Floury-2', are much richer in lysine than other strains. Hybrids, such as triticale (wheat X rye), also have great advantages from the nutritional standpoint. Finally, it has already been mentioned that selection can produce rapeseed without erucic acid and without goitrogenic substances. All these techniques, however, must always be carefully tested and checked, as are all the other techniques aimed at protecting crops and animals and at preventing changes occurring in the products obtained from such crops and animals either directly or after processing.

In this connection, there is constant exchange of information between the World Health Organization (WHO), the Food and Agriculture Organization of the United Nations (FAO) and the Protein Calorie Advisory Group of the United Nations (PAG)[1], the health and agricultural authorities of each country and also between, or with, the manufacturers of products destined for agriculture or for use as food additives. The monographs prepared by FAO and WHO before committee meetings are sent to the interested parties, including manufacturers, for their comments. Most of the regulations drawn up in the various countries, or in the EEC, are based on FAO/WHO recommendations.

The way in which the consumer is protected at the international level will be covered in the next section, which is based largely on an article by Kermode and McNally (1973), which appeared in a special edition of FAO's *Nutrition News* published for the 25th anniversary of WHO.

Recommendations of international bodies

JOINT FAO/WHO FOOD STANDARDS PROGRAMME —
CODEX ALIMENTARIUS COMMISSION

In the introduction to the special edition of *Nutrition News* mentioned above (Kermode and McNally, 1973), M. Ganzin, former Director of FAO's Food Policy and Nutrition Division, writes that the Codex Alimentarius, which was started jointly by FAO and WHO, is a good illustration of the "positive and fruitful collaboration between the organizations in the service of all the Member Nations of FAO and WHO."

---

[1] As mentioned previously, on 1 January 1978, PAG was replaced by a new body consisting of a Sub-Committee on Nutrition (SCN) of the United Nations Administrative Coordination Committee with technical support from the Advisory Group of Nutrition (AGN).

Attempts have always been made to protect the interests and health of consumers both at the national level, i.e., domestically produced goods, and as regards imported products, in order to ensure a supply of products that are both safe and of good quality. It has been essential, therefore, to try to establish international food standards to achieve these goals so that exporters can know what is required of them and importers can explicitly state their general and specific requirements.

However, progress in this field has been very slow, at least until the end of the Second World War. It should be stressed that it is impossible to facilitate trade between countries by lowering trade barriers without first harmonizing national food standards. Without this, there is a risk of permitting technical barriers to remain in place of customs barriers. The end result is exactly the same. In drawing up a general agreement on technical problems, understanding can be reached on a great variety of questions related to the protection of the consumer's health, e.g., maximum levels for certain contaminants, whether natural or resulting from processing, acceptable daily intakes, etc. In 1958, an FAO committee of government experts, working in liaison with the International Dairy Federation, began to draw up a code of principles concerning milk and milk products as well as compositional standards for the latter. This considerable body of work was the result of close cooperation among the different governments so that, by taking their various observations into account, standards could eventually be established.

This was the first FAO/WHO step toward the drawing up of international food standards. Another was at the initiative of Dr H. Frenzel, of Austria, which resulted in the setting up of a body known as the "Codex Alimentarius Europaeus."

Created jointly by the International Commission of Agricultural Industries and the Permanent Bureau of Analytical Chemistry (and despite various difficulties in the early stages), the Codex Alimentarius Europaeus proposed, in 1962, that its work should be taken over by FAO and WHO. The governing bodies of these international organizations then gave approval for the setting up, under their joint patronage, of the Codex Alimentarius Commission. In 1962, an inaugural Conference on Food Standards laid down guidelines for the first session of the Codex Alimentarius Commission, which began work some months later, in 1963, with the approval of the 11th Conference of FAO and the 16th World Health Assembly. Some 30 countries took part in the first session. Since then the number of attending countries has grown to 117. Close to two thirds of these are developing countries, very few of which were, at the beginning, members of the Codex Alimentarius Commission.

What are the objectives and scope of Codex Alimentarius?

The Codex Alimentarius [1] "is a collection of internationally adopted food standards presented in a uniform manner." These food standards aim at protecting consumers' health and ensuring fair practices in the food trade. The Codex Alimentarius also includes provisions of an advisory nature in the form of codes of practice, guidelines and other recommended measures intended to assist in achieving the purposes of the Codex Alimentarius. The publication of the Codex Alimentarius is intended to guide and promote the elaboration and the establishment of definitions and requirements to assist in their harmonization and in doing so to facilitate international trade.

"The Codex Alimentarius includes standards for all the principal foods, whether processed, semi-processed or raw, for distribution to the consumer. Materials for further processing into foods should be included to the extent necessary to achieve the purposes of the Codex Alimentarius as defined. There are 23 subsidiary bodies of which 3 are concerned with general policy, 6 with general matters applicable to all foods and 15 with matters applicable to specific groups of foods.

"The Codex Alimentarius includes provisions in respect of food hygiene, food additives, pesticide residues, contaminants, labelling and presentation, methods of analysis and sampling. It also includes provisions of an advisory nature in the form of codes of practice, guidelines and other recommended measures.

"A Codex standard for any food is drawn up in accordance with the Format for Codex Commodity Standards and contains, as appropriate, the criteria listed therein."

A country accepts a Codex standard − in respect of distribution of the product concerned, whether imported or home-produced, within its territorial jurisdiction − in the following ways:

● Full acceptance;
● Target acceptance within a stated number of years but in the meantime not hindering, by any legal or administrative provisions, the distribution within its territorial jurisdiction of any sound products conforming to standards;
● Acceptance with deviations, provided such deviations and the reasons for them are specified.

A country that considers it cannot accept the standard in any of the ways mentioned above must indicate "in what way its present or proposed re-

---

[1] According to the General Principles of the Codex Alimentarius Commission (4th edition of the Procedural Manual of the Codex Alimentarius Commission).

quirements differ from the standard, and, if possible the reasons for these differences." It must also state whether products conforming to the standards of Codex Alimentarius may be distributed freely within its territorial jurisdiction.

Up to now the Codex Alimentarius Commission has already adopted 103 international standards, and 115 countries have accepted the standards sent to their governments for approval.

It seems, however, that these standards are aimed first of all at encouraging the safe use of food additives, pesticides and their residues, the acceptable daily intakes (ADI) of which are established by toxicologists. In the area of food additives, a detailed study has been made by Bigwood and Gérard (1971; see Figure 7). The doses have been studied for each product, additive or pesticide concerned. However, it is difficult, at this stage, to determine what the result of their cumulative or synergistic action might be. It is as if it had been decided, quite rightly, to study first what is added every day to simple foods as a result of advances in the techniques used in agriculture and in the food industry. This is perfectly understandable. It was noted at the beginning of this book that "natural" foods were, in principle, looked upon favourably. It is worth noting, however, that the harmful substances in these natural foods are becoming better known and a list of them is being completed and kept up to date. In many countries, tolerance limits have been proposed for these undesirable substances. Such is the case with aflatoxins, at least in the EEC. However, unanimity is not always found in the framework of restricted international organizations such as the EEC. It would often be easier for such organizations just to adopt the standards of the Codex Alimentarius, considering that the different governments have a sufficient period of time for consideration before accepting them.

At present there are, as mentioned earlier, 23 subsidiary bodies of the Codex Alimentarius Commission. These are listed in the annexes to the article by Kermode and McNally (1973). Some of these committees are concerned with simple products and their derivatives: milk and milk products; meat and processed meat products; fish and fishery products and subjects such as meat hygiene. Other committees are responsible for the elaboration of standards relating to foods for special dietary uses, food additives, food hygiene in general, or general principles of the Codex. It is just as important to standardize these principles as it is to standardize the procedures for the acceptance of standards. It is also essential to establish criteria of priority and, finally, to define the terms used in the Codex Alimentarius.

After years of intensive study and careful reflection (such an undertaking cannot be rushed), the current trend is to give increasing weight to the

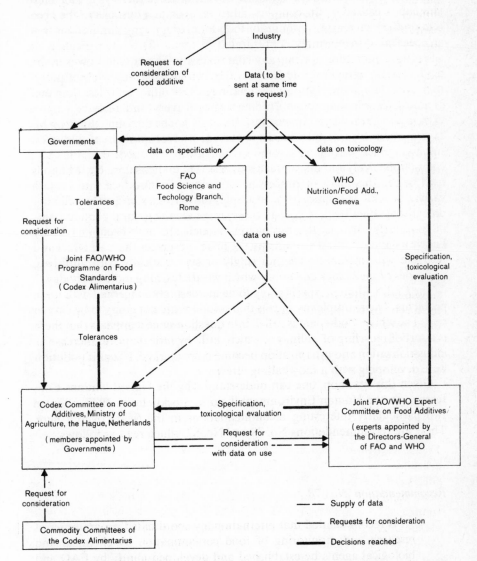

FIGURE 7. Flow diagram for international acceptance of food additives. (Taken from FAO Nutrition Meetings Report No. 40.)

problems of environmental contamination and, consequently, to food contamination caused by the complex industrial evolution of society. The need
is to produce increasing amounts of food for ever-growing populations that
are becoming increasingly concentrated in towns. The intensification of
agriculture, therefore, appears as a vital necessity. This entails, however, the
use of certain agricultural techniques that can increase the levels of pollution, even though the pollution originating in agriculture is far less than that
of industrial or human origin. Human wastes of every kind, including man's
excreta, are a real danger for ecology. It should not be forgotten that with his
excreta man diffuses into the environment a great number of additives,
sulphonamides, antibiotics (some of which are not biodegradable, e.g.,
chloramphenicol) and microorganisms resistant to medicines, etc. Methods
used in the treatment or processing of foodstuffs introduce into these a
variety of toxic substances: for example, nitrosamines and polycyclic hydrocarbons. Finally, on top of all these, there are the natural contaminants
of foodstuffs, such as the mycotoxins (which are now becoming better
known) and the natural antinutritive or toxic substances that can affect and
interfere with metabolism either singly or synergistically with additives,
pesticides or medicines and about which we are learning more every day.

The Codex Alimentarius is going to be increasingly concerned with these
problems. Their complexity means that solutions are not going to be easy to
find. The whole food-chain is called into question since it appears that there
is a sort of recycling of pollution, which, little by little, tends to increase as
industrialization and urbanization become more marked. It is as if pollution
were developing with a snowballing effect.

Given this situation, one can understand why the United Nations Conference on the Human Environment, held in Stockholm in 1972, adopted
two particularly interesting recommendations in the field covered here.
These are recommendations No. 78 and No. 82, which read as follows:

Recommendation No. 78

"It is recommended that internationally coordinated programmes of
research and monitoring of food contamination by chemical and
biological agents be established and developed jointly by FAO and
WHO, taking into account national programmes, and that the results
of monitoring be expeditiously assembled, evaluated and made
available so as to provide early information on rising trends of contamination and on levels that may be considered undesirable or may
lead to unsafe human intakes."

Recommendation No. 82

"It is recommended that increased support be given to the Codex Alimentarius Commission to develop international standards for pollutants in food and a Code of Ethics for international food trade, and that the capabilities of the Food and Agriculture Organization of the United Nations and the World Health Organization in the field of food control be increased."

Attention should be drawn to one essential point. Whatever is undesirable for some is undesirable for all. It is unacceptable that something should be tolerated for some and forbidden for others. Of course, there are some agricultural imperatives that are closely linked to the vital needs of populations in developing countries, but it would seem perfectly logical, and possible, for these imperatives and needs to be reconciled.

In their evaluations and recommendations, Codex committees quite rightly pay a great deal of attention to data on health as well as data on agriculture. They also look at the order of priorities "in which additives and pesticides have to be evaluated or re-evaluated," and forward recommendations to the Joint FAO/WHO Expert Committee on Food Additives and to the Joint FAO/WHO Meeting on Pesticide Residues, respectively, regarding their future programme of action. Priorities are established on the basis of the hazards that the products studied could pose as well as their interaction with food products. Thus, for example, the Joint FAO/WHO Expert Committee on Food Additives warned, in its fourteenth report, that trichloroethylene (used in the decaffeination of coffee) reacts with cystine in proteins to give a compound, the toxicological study of which was not considered adequate despite the negative results obtained. As a result of these reports extra precautions were taken in several countries. This example, which is but one of many, shows that nothing is left to chance.

In particular, potential daily intakes are nearly always overestimated. In spite of these precautions, as Lu (1974) has stressed, they can still sometimes be underestimated, since they are calculated on average food consumption. It could thus well be, particularly in the case of additives used in confectionery and drinks, that certain people ingest quantities well in excess not only of the average intake of the population, but even of the intake of consumers with a high rate of consumption. Such underestimates can have tragic consequences. This was the case with the addition of cobaltous salts to beer. In certain countries, the authorities were informed that the average beer intake of drinkers was four litres a day. Then, numerous cases of cardiac disease began to be reported, some of them fatal, which occurred after drinking this beer. Even though there were other concomitant factors, an inquiry still revealed that all the persons affected had drunk the suspect beer in quantities that were many times greater than the average [1].

Of course it is obvious that it is very difficult to allow for extraordinary food or drinking habits or for plain greediness, which, in some cases, is nothing more than sheer gluttony. Abnormal eating and drinking kill.

In the case of pesticide residues or growth promoters, such risks practically do not exist. More and more users tend not to exaggerate. As regards animal feedstuffs, controls show that regulations are complied with. When they are not observed it is generally a case of underdosage for economic reasons, and this is easy to detect. Educational programmes, which still have to be expanded and improved, help the producers to understand and accept their responsibilities.

Thus, at the highest international level, recommendations based on studies, investigations and controls allow for the various risks run by the consumer to be examined in relation to his overall diet. These recommendations are given concrete form through accelerated procedures and, where necessary, adapted to the needs of advances in agriculture and health protection.

Nevertheless, as mentioned above and despite the trend now developing, certain antinutritive substances in natural foods have been somewhat neglected. Of course, antitrypsins, haemagglutinins, antithyroids, oestrogens, mineral-chelating agents and the antivitamins have all been the subjects of basic and applied research both in animal husbandry and, when events made it essential to do so, also in human nutrition. Such was the case with phytic acid in cereals used in baking during the Second World War. Sometimes the interaction of food consumption and therapy has led to a closer examination of certain problems, such as those concerning the relationship between toxic amines and monoamine oxidase inhibitors. There is no need to mention favism, lathyrism or other, similar illnesses, the origins of which are now well known. These are dealt with in a different way and success will increase with the growing desire to produce more protein-rich grain legumes and, using these as raw materials, to produce textured protein as the basis of new, non-traditional food.

It is within this context that the United Nations Protein and Calorie Advisory Group (PAG) elaborated certain recommendations that were taken up by the Codex Alimentarius Commission. PAG requested experts to examine what methods, whether agricultural or technological, or both, could be used to achieve the complete removal of undesirable natural

---

[1] Yet cobalt is one of the trace elements essential for life. It is part of the Vitamin B_{12} molecule, where it is found in amounts of around 4.54 percent. As has been frequently said, there are no toxic substances, there are only toxic doses.

substances that might be harmful, and that might reduce the consumption of foodstuffs capable of providing man's protein requirements; this is especially important in the context of the current world situation of a worrying increase in populations and urbanization (see p. 125).

Conclusions

Despite these efforts and the significant progress made, the public, even an informed public of doctors and health workers, is still often ignorant of the effects of antinutritive substances in natural food and pays far too much attention to the question of food additives. It is true that the public is encouraged in this by environmental activists, whose motives are not always entirely disinterested. Quite apart from all the regulations based on solid, internationally established norms, which are the sources for national legislation, there always seem to be certain psychoses pertaining to food and nutrition [1]. We will conclude by reiterating these psychoses in an attempt to show how inane they are.

The myth of the "natural" disguises some realities and these include the dangers that exist in some foods that are used every day. Pirie (1969) has pointed out that few subjects give rise to so many myths as food, illness and gardening. He could have added that food and illness, and even food and gardening are often linked together in the minds of many people and this reinforces the food myth and a growing distrust of anything that is not familiar. The consumer forgets the precautions taken to protect and inform him. In fact, the way things are, it is as if there were a deliberate conspiracy to keep him unaware of these precautions. The results of quite a considerable amount of work (often thankless) done by national and international bodies to protect the consumer are not at all sufficiently well known or explained. Bigwood and Gérard (1971) feel that the consumer's knowledge depends on his ability to understand and interpret correctly the information given to him. In order to improve this knowledge it is essential to have continuity; but this continuity must come from informed and impartial specialists who should not be afraid, as the previously mentioned authors have put it, of making news out of information that, if spread by the uninformed, could be slanted. Perhaps in this way it could be possible to counteract the activities of those whom one should not hesitate to describe as real psychopaths and exploiters of pollution: those who can rally hordes

---

[1] For example, in the EEC, there are as many as three scientific committees: one for human food, another for animal food and a third for pesticides.

of willing innocents to their cause and who are nostalgic for the old methods of agriculture to which the population explosion has made it absolutely impossible for the world to return.

Biraben (1974) reminds us that the present world population growth rate is about 2 percent per year; this, in 170 years, would result in a world population of 155.8 thousand million people (one inhabitant for each square metre). He then points out that if the present global birth rate is maintained (about 37 per 1 000), and mortality continues to decline at the current rate (reaching, around 1990, the level found in the developed countries), the annual growth rate will become nearly 3 percent and the number of 135 thousand million could be reached in 135 or 140 years. The above author adds that the demographic problem is certainly the most serious of our time and wonders if it can be solved without a crisis. This is the challenge that faces us.

Urbanization and the flight from the land render the problem even more difficult. The consumer must be made to realize that it is all connected with his food. One cannot, in fact, isolate demography from food, traditional and non-traditional, and the current conditions of agricultural production. The following facts should help us to reflect on this question:

- Taking only 17 food-, fodder- and oil-producing plants, the experts have calculated that, in order to get the total outputs for 1968-70 with the yields of 30 years previously, it would have been necessary to bring an extra 150 million hectares under cultivation;
- Losses caused by insects, plant disease and weeds vary between 15 and 35 percent of the total harvest;
- In recent years, India has imported quantities of cereals simply to compensate for what has been destroyed by insects and pests (it is known that six rats eat as much as a single man). Here we are only talking about the quantities involved. We have already seen what has to be said on the question of quality.

These examples could be multiplied. The specialists are aware of them; the public, which has forgotten whatever it once knew of agriculture, is ignorant of them and there are many people who seem bent on making the public more and more ignorant. Von Pufendorf (1974) has written that if we want agriculture to fulfil its essential function of feeding mankind while still protecting our environment, then it will be necessary to have recourse not only to practical and structural methods but also to new socio-cultural concepts. It would be hard to stress enough how essential it is, and, at the same time, urgent, to harmonize industrial civilization with intensive agricultural production and to accustom people to the idea of using non-traditional foods.

To achieve this, the results of the work done by the Codex Alimentarius Commission should be better publicized in circles outside those connected with its work. The nutritional sciences should also be given the recognition they deserve but that is often denied to them either through ignorance or negligence. To achieve this position, however, would imply that numerous industrial and research activities, as well as teaching, would have to be completely re-evaluated in the light of their economic and technological efficiency, by confronting them with the growing imperatives of the world's food requirements.

BIBLIOGRAPHY

ADAMIYA, A. *Akad. Nauk Graz. SSR*, 64: 237.
1971
ADRIAN, J. *Annls Nutr. Aliment.*, 17: 1.
1963
ADRIAN, J. *Annls Nutr. Aliment.*, 19: 27.
1965
ADRIAN, J. & FAVIER, J.C. *Annls Nutr. Aliment.*, 15: 181.
1961
ALBANO-ANNICHINO, G., INTRIERI, F. & ZICARELLI, L. *Atti Soc. ital. Sci. vet.*, 26: 394.
1972
ALEXANDER, G. & ROSSITER, J. *Aust. J. agric. Res.*, 3: 24.
1952
ALTHOFF, J.D. *Medsche Klin.*, 65: 1204.
1970
AMBROSE, A.M., COX, A.J. & DE EDS, F. *J. agric. Fd Chem.*, 6: 600.
1958
ANSON, M.L. & PADER, M. *Method for preparing a meat-like product.* US Patent 2879: 163.
1959
APPLEBAUM, S.W., SHLOMO, M. & BIRK, Y. *J. agric. Fd Chem.*, 17: 618.
1969
ARCHER, DANIELS, MIDLAND COMPANY. Bulletin 1126.
1967
ARRHENIUS, E. *Ambio*, 2: 49.
1973
ASPINALL, G.O., BEGBIE, R. & MCKAY, J.E. *Cereal Science Today*, 12: 223.
1967
ATTREP, K.A., MARIANI, I.M. JR. & ATTREP, M. JR. *Lipids*, 8: 484.
1973
AYHAN, I.H. & KAYAALP, S.O. *Ankara Univ. Tip. Fak. Mecm.*, 24: 531.
1971
BAGNIS, R., BERGLUND, F., ELIAS, P.S., ESCH, J.G. VAN, HAKSTEAD, B.W. & KOJIMA, K.
1970   Problems of toxicants in marine food products. 1. Marine biotoxins. *Bull. Wld Hlth Org.*, 42: 69-88.
BANDYOPADHYAY, G.C. *Diss. Abstr. Int.*, 31: 3090B.
1970
BASLOW, M.H. *Marine pharmacology.* Baltimore, Williams and Wilkins.
1969
BAZELL, R.J. *Science, N.Y.*, 174: 574.
1971
BELL, R.R., DRAPER, H.H. & BERGAN, J.C. *Am. J. clin. Nutr.*, 26: 1185.
1973

BENDER, A. J. Fd Technol., 1: 261.
1966
BENEVENGA, N.J. J. agric. Fd Chem., 21.
1973
BENEVENGA, N.J. J. agric. Fd Chem., 22: 2.
1974
BENNETS, H.W., UNDERWOOD, E.J. & SHIER, F.L. Aust. vet. J., 22: 2.
1946
BERK, J.E. Ann. N.Y. Acad. Sci., 150: 1.
1968
BERTRAND, G. C.r hebd. Séanc. Acad. Sci., Paris, 143: 832.
1906
BESSMO, H. & KUROSAWA, S. J. Jap. Soc. Fd Nutr., 20: 314.
1967
BICKOFF, E.M. Amer. Perfum. Cosmet., 83: 59, 64.
1968
BICKOFF, E.M. & KOHLER, G.O. PAG Bull., 3: 19.
1973
BIGWOOD, E.J. & GÉRARD, A. Objectifs et principes fondamentaux d'un droit comparé de
1971   l'alimentation. 4 vols. Bâle, Karger.
BIRABEN, J.N. Etudes, p. 337.
1974
BIROLAUD, P. Les levures, aliments sources de protéines. Document, Neuvième Symposium
1968   international sur les sources de protéines dans l'alimentation humaine, Amsterdam,
          1968, p. 182-201.
BIZZI, A., TACCONI, E., VENERONI, A.J., SALMONA, G., DE GAETANO, G., PAGLIALUNGA, S. &
1976   GARATTINI, S. Biological significance of the accumulation of uneven fatty acids in
          various animal species fed with diets containing SCP. Milan, Istituto Mario Negri.
BLEUMINK, E. Wld Rev. Nutr. Diet., 12: 505.
1970
BOENICKE, R. & CZOK, G. Quatrième Colloque Inst. chim. cafés verts et torréfiés et dérivés, Paris,
1970   1969: 209.
BOGOVSKI, P., CASTEGNARO, M., PIGNATELLI, B. & WALKER, E.A. Proc. Work Conf., 1971: 127.
1972   Lyons, International Agency for Research on Cancer.
BOMBAL, J., N'DIAYE, A.L., FENARDJI, F. & FERRANDO, R. Rev. Méd. vét., 128: 469.
1974
BORIES, G. & TULLIEZ, J. Les hydrocarbures aliphatiques des algues spirulines: nature, étude de
1973   leur métabolisme chez le rat. Colloque sur la valeur nutritionnelle des algues spiru-
          lines. Paris, DGRST and Institut français du pétrole.
BOTTINI, E., LUCARELLI, P., AGOSTINO, R., PALMARINO, R., BUSIUCO, L. & ANTGUONI, G.
1971   Science, N.Y., 171: 409.
BOVAY, E. Trav. chim. aliment. Hyg., 61: 303.
1970
BOVAY, E., HOFMANN, W., ZUBER, R., KUPFER, U., GISIGER, L. & BLANC, B. Rech. agron. suisse,
1970   9 (fasc. 2): 159.
BOYD, C.E. Econ. Bot., 22: 359.
1968
BOYD, C.E. Econ. Bot., 23: 123.
1969
BOYER, R.A. High protein food product and process for its preparation. US Patent, 1954, 2, 682,
1954, 1959   447. US Patent, 1959, 2, 730, 466.

BOYER, R.A. & SAEWERT, H.E. *US Patent 543,716, 16 July 1956.*
1956
BOYLAND, E. *Tumori,* 53: 19.
1967
BRETH, F.E. *Rev. Elev.,* 24: 91.
1969
BRIEGER, L. *Virchows Arch. path. Anat. Physiol.,* 112: 549.
1888
BRIEGER, L. *Virchows Arch. path. Anat. Physiol.,* 115: 483.
1889
BURGOS, A., CAVINESS, C.E., FLOYD, J.I. & STEPHENSON, E.L. *Poultry Sci.,* 52: 1822.
1973
BURKET, R.E. Protein markets for 1972. *Soybean Dig.,* 31: 6.
1971
BURRELL, R.J.W., ROACH, W.A. & SCHADWELL, A. *J. natn. Cancer Inst.,* 36: 201.
1966
CAHNMANN, H.J. & KURATSUNE, M. *Analyt. Chem.,* 29: 1312.
1957
CALET, C. *Perspectives en matière d'alimentation des volailles. Cycles d'études.* Vol. 3. Paris,
1968   Flammarion.
CALLOWAY, D.H. Gas in the alimentary canal. In *Handbook of physiology.* Section 6. *Aliment-*
1968   *ary canal.* Vol. 5, Chap. 137, p. 2839. Baltimore, Md, Williams and Wilkins.
CALLOWAY, D.H. Gas forming property of food legumes. *In* Protein-Calorie Advisory Group
1973   of the United Nations System. *Nutritional improvement of food legumes by breed-*
        ing ... New York, United Nations.
CHAMPAGNAT, A. & ADRIAN, J. *Pétrole et protéines.* Paris, Doin.
1974
CHEEKE, P.R. & MYER, R.O. *Feedstuffs,* 45: 24.
1973
Chem. Engng News, 29 October: 19.
1973
Chem. Engng News, 18 February: 20.
1974a
Chem. Engng News, 15 April: 25.
1974b
CHEN, K.K., FLEMING, W.J. & LIN, T.M. *J. Pharm.,* 134: 435.
1961
CHEN, LAN-BO & ISSENBERG, P. *J. agric. Fd Chem.,* 20: 113.
1972
CHEYMOL, J. *Avanc. Sciences,* 2: 3.
1970
CHICHESTER, C.O. *Wld Rev. Nutr. Diet.,* 16: 318.
1973
CLEMENT, G., GIDDEY, C. & MENZI, R. *J. Sci. Fd Agric.,* 18: 497.
1967
CLEMENTS, F.W. *Br. med. Bull.,* 16: 133.
1960
CLEMENTS, F.W. & WISHART, J.W. *Metabolism,* 5: 623.
1956
CONTOUR, S. *Ind. aliment. agric.,* 87: 225.
1970

CONTOUR, S. & GUBLER, D. *Ind. aliment. agric.*, 72.
1972

COUCH, J.R., CREGER, C.R. & BAKSHI, Y.K. *Proc. Soc. exp. Biol. Med.*, 123: 263.
1966

COULSON, E.J., REMINGTON, R.E. & LYNCH, K.M. *J. Nutr.*, 10: 255.
1935

COUSINS, R.J., BARBER, A.K. & TROUT, J.R. *J. Nutr.*, 103: 964.
1973

COWAN, J.W., SAGHIR, A.R. & SALJI, J.P. *Aust. J. biol. Sci.*, 20: 683.
1967

CUNHA, T.J. *Feedstuffs*, 42: 22.
1970

CURLEY, A., VINCENT, A., SEDLAK, E.F., GIRLING, R.E., HAWK, R.E. & BARTHEL, W.F. *Science,*
1971   *N.Y.*, 172: 65.

DAHAN, J.R. *Ind. aliment. agric.*, 6: 35.
1973

DANIEL, L.J. *Nutr. Abstr. Rev.*, 31: 1.
1961

DAVYS, M.N.G. & PIRIE, N.W. *J. agric. engng Res.*, 6: 71.
1963

DE CRÉMIERS, P. & MAUBRAS, Y. *Filière technico-économique du soja.* Paris, Institut national de
1972   la recherche agronomique.

DE FREMERY, D., MILLER, R.E., EDWARDS, R.H., KNUCKLES, B.E., BICKOFF, E.M. & KOHLER,
1973   G.O. *J. agric. Fd Chem.*, 21: 886.

DE GROOT, A.P. & SHUMP, P. *J. Nutr.*, 98: 45.
1969

DE GROOT, A.P., TIL, H.P. & FERON, V.J. *Fd Cosmet. Toxicol.*, 9: 787.
1971

DE GROOT, A.P., SHUMP, P., FERON, V.J. & VAN BEEK, L. *J. Nutr.*, 106: 1527.
1976

DELEZENNE, C. & POZERSKY, E. *C.r. Séanc. Soc. Biol.*, 55: 935.
1903

D'ELME, P. Le pouvoir des consommateurs. *Etudes*, p. 537.
1973

DE RENZO, E.C., MCKERNS, K.W., BIRD, H.H., CEKLENIAK, W.P., COULOMB, B. & KALEITA, E.
1959   *Biochem. Pharmac.*, 1: 236.

DISSANAYADE, A.S., TRUELOVE, S.C., OFFORD, R. & WHITEHEAD, R. *Lancet*, 2: 709.
1973

D'MELLO, J.P.F. *Br. Poultry Sci.*, 14: 291.
1973a

D'MELLO, J.P.F. *Nutr. Rep. Int.*, 8: 105.
1973b

DOHRN, M., FAURE, W. & BLOREVOGEL, W. *Medsche Klin.*, 22: 1417.
1926

DOKTOROVICH, M.A. *Svinovodstvo*, (9): 44.
1969

DORAISWAMY, T.R., SINGH, N. & DANIEL, V.A. *Br. J. Nutr.*, 23: 737.
1969

DOROGOPLYA, A.G., MYASNIKOV, A.I., ZHIRNOVA, N.E. & NINICHENKO, A.N. *Vop. Onkol.*, 18:
1972   70.

DRIEUX, H., FERRANDO, R. & JACQUOT, R. *Caractéristiques alimentaires de la viande de bou-*
1962   *cherie.* Paris, Vigot.
DUNSTAN, W.R. & HENRY, T.A. *Proc. R. Soc., Ser. B,* 72: 285.
1903
EAKIN, E.R., SNELL, E.E. & WILLIAMS, J.R. *J. biol. Chem.,* 136: 801.
1940a
EAKIN, E.R., SNELL, E.E. & WILLIAMS, J.R. *Science, N.Y.,* 92: 224.
1940b
EAKIN, E.R., SNELL, E.E. & WILLIAMS, J.R. *J. biol. Chem.,* 140: 535.
1941
EHRHARDT, J.P. *Annls falsif. Expert. chim.,* 64: 100.
1971
EKLUND, A. *Nutr. Rep. Int.,* 7: 647.
1973
EL-KARIMI, M.M.A & HILMY MEHDI, I. *Ann. Coll. Méd. Mosul, Nouv., sér.,* 2: 23.
1971
ELMADFA, I. & MENDEN, E. Z. *Lebensmittelsunters. u. -Forsch.,* 152: 340.
1973
ENGEL, C. Analyse des essais toxicologiques effectués sur les levures cultivées sur alcanes. In
1972   *Les levures cultivées sur alcanes. Symposium d'Aix-en-Provence,* ed by H. Gounelle
           de Pontanel. Paris, Centre de recherches Foch.
ENGST, R. *Scr. med.. Fac. med. Univ. Brun Purkynianae,* 46: 79.
1973
ESCHER, F.E., KOEHLER, P.E. & AYRES, J.C. *Appl. Microbiol.,* 26: 27.
1973
EVANS, R.J. & JACK, D.B. *Environ. Sci. Technol.,* 6: 901.
1972
FAIRBAIRN, J.W., ed. *The pharmacology of plant phenolics. Proceedings.* New York and Lon-
1959   don, Academic Press.
FAO. *Protein requirements: report of a Joint FAO/WHO Expert Group.* Rome. FAO Nutrition
1965   Meetings Report Series 37.
FAO. *Technology of production of edible flours and protein products from soybean,* by S.S. De.
1971   Rome. Agricultural Services Bulletin No. 11.
FAO/WHO. *Evaluation of the carcinogenic hazards of food additives: fifth report of the Joint*
1961   *FAO/WHO Expert Committee on Food Additives.* Rome. Nutrition Meetings Re-
           port Series No. 29; Geneva. Technical Report Series 220.
FAO/WHO. *Evaluation of the toxicity of a number of antimicrobials and antioxidants: sixth*
1962   *report of the Joint FAO/WHO Expert Committee on Food Additives.* Rome. Nutri-
           tion Meetings Report Series No. 31; Geneva. Technical Report Series 228.
FAO/WHO. *Specifications for the identity and purity of food additives and their toxicological*
1965   *evaluation; food colours and some antimicrobials and antioxidants: eighth report of*
           the Joint FAO/WHO Expert Committee on Food Additives. Rome. Nutrition Meet-
           ings Report Series No. 38; Geneva. Technical Report Series 309.
FAO/WHO. *Specifications for the identity and purity of food additives and their toxicological*
1966   *evaluation; some antimicrobials, antioxidants, emulsifiers, stabilizers, flour-treatment*
           agents, acids and bases: ninth report of the Joint FAO/WHO Expert Committee
           on Food Additives. Rome. Nutrition Meetings Report Series No. 40; Geneva. Techni-
           cal Report Series 339.
FAO/WHO. *Specifications for the identity and purity of food additives and their toxicological*
1969   *evaluation; some antibiotics: twelfth report of the Joint FAO/WHO Expert Com-*

mittee on Food Additives. Rome. Nutrition Meetings Report Series No. 45; Geneva. Technical Report Series 430.

FAO/WHO. *Specifications for the identity and purity of food additives and their toxicological*
1970 *evaluation; some food colours, emulsifiers, stabilizers, anti-caking agents, and certain other substances: thirteenth report of the Joint FAO/WHO Expert Committee on Food Additives*. Rome. Nutrition Meetings Report Series No. 46; Geneva. Technical Report Series 445.

FAO/WHO. *Pesticide residues in food: report of the Joint Meeting of the FAO Working Party of*
1969-73 *Experts on Pesticide Residues and the WHO Expert Committee on Pesticide Residues, 1968-72*. Rome. FAO Agricultural Studies Nos. 78, 84, 87, 88, 90; Geneva. Technical Report Series 417, 458, 474, 502, 525.

FAO/WHO. *Evaluation of certain food additives and the contaminants mercury, lead and*
1972 *cadmium*: sixteenth report of the Joint FAO/WHO Expert Committee on Food Additives. Rome. Nutrition Meetings Report Series No. 51; Geneva. Technical Report Series 505.

FAZIO, T., WHITE, R.H., DUSOLD, L.R. & HOWARD, J.W. *J. Ass. off. anal. Chem.*, 56: 919.
1973

FEIGEN, G.A., SANZ, E. & ALENDER, C.B. *Toxicon.*, 4: 161.
1966

FELLNER, O.O. *Medsche Klin.*, 22: 1886.
1926

FENG, P.G. & KEAN, E.A. *Br. J. Nutr.*, 9: 368.
1955

FENSELAU, C. & TALALAY, P. *Fd Cosmet. Toxicol.*, 11: 597.
1973

FERRANDO, R. *Revue Path. comp. Hyg. gén.*, 49: 579.
1949

FERRANDO, R. *Alimentation et équilibre biologique*. Paris, Flammarion.
1961

FERRANDO, R. *Voeding*, 30: 447.
1969

FERRANDO, R. *Annls Nutr. Aliment.*, 25: 145.
1970

FERRANDO, R. *Annls Nutr. Aliment.*, 25: B231-B375.
1971

FERRANDO, R. L'hygiéniste face aux aliments conventionnels et non conventionnels. In *Les*
1972a *levures cultivées sur alcanes. Symposium d'Aix-en-Provence*, ed by H. Gounelle de Pontanel. Paris, Centre de recherches Foch.

FERRANDO, R. *Riv. ital. Sostanze grasse*, 49: 73.
1972b

FERRANDO, R. & RATSIMAMANGA, A.R. *Annls Nutr. Aliment.*, 14: 31.
1960

FERRANDO, R. & SPAÏS, A. *Proc. 7th Int. Congr. Nutr., Hamburg*, p. 276.
1966

FERRANDO, R. & MAINGUY, P. *Annls Nutr. Aliment.*, 24: B445.
1970

FERRANDO, R. & TRUHAUT, R. *C.r. hebd. Séanc. Acad. Sci., Paris, sér. D*, 275: 279.
1972a

FERRANDO, R. & TRUHAUT, R. *C.r. hebd. Séanc. Acad. Sci., Paris, sér. D*, 275: 587.
1972b

FERRANDO, R. & N'DIAYE, A.L. *Annls Nutr. Aliment.*, 27: 11.
1973

FERRANDO, R., BOISSELOT-LEFEBVRE, J. & RATSIMAMANGA, A.R. *C.r. Séanc. Soc. Biol.*, 154:
1960a 579.

FERRANDO, R., BOISSELOT-LEFEBVRE, J. & RATSIMAMANGA, A.R. Répercussions possibles de la
1960b présence d'hormones dans le régime, en particulier dans le lait, sur la physiologie de
la nutrition. *Proc. 5th Int. Congr. Nutr., Washington, 1960.*

FERRANDO, R., GUILLEUX, M.M. & GUÉRILLOT-VINET, A. *Nature, Lond.*, 192: 1205.
1961

FERRANDO, R., PARODI, A., HENRY, N., DELFORT-LAVAL, J. & N'DIAYE, A.L. *C.r. Acad. Sci.*,
1977 *Páris, sér. D*, 284: 855.

FESTENSTEIN, G.N. *J. Sci. Fd Agric.*, 12: 305.
1961

FORNAL, J., FORNAL, L. & BABUCHOWSKI, K. *Pregl-Zbozowomlyn.*, 14: 445.
1970

FREIMUTH, U. & GLÄSER, E. *Nahrung*, 14: 357.
1970

GABEL, W. & KRUGER, W. *Mün. med. Wschr.*, 67: 214.
1920

GARKAVAYA, V.V. & RAMANIS, U. *Latv. Lopkopibas Vet. Zinat. Petnieciska Inst. Ruksti*, 26: 41.
1971a

GARKAVAYA, V.V. & RAMANIS, U. *Nauka Zhivotnovod.*, 1971 (10): 41.
1971b

GARRIGUES, R. *Arch. Biol. méd.*, 33: 1737.
1957

GENEVOIS, L. *Mutations biochimiques chez les végétaux supérieurs.* Paris, Masson.
1973

GENIGEORGIS, C.A. & RIEMANN, H. *Wld Rev. Nutr. Diet.*, 16: 364.
1973

GERRARD, J.W., LUBOS, M.C., HARDY, L.W., HOLMUND, B.A. & WEBSTER, D. *Can. med. Ass. J.*,
1967 97: 780.

GILBERT, E.F. & PISTEY, W. *J. Reprod. Fert.*, 34: 495.
1973

GMELIN, R. & VIRTANEN, A.I. *Acta chem. scand.*, 13: 1474, 1718; 14: 507.
1959-60

GOLDBLATT, L.A. *Aflatoxin.* New York and London, Academic Press.
1969

GOLDMAN, A.S., ANDERSON, D.W., SELLARS, W.A., SAPERSTEIN, S., KNIKER, W.T. & HALPERN,
1963 S.R. *Pediatrics*, 32: 425.

GONTZEA, I., FERRANDO, R. & SUTZESCO, P. *Substances antinutritives des aliments naturels.*
1968 Paris, Vigot.

GORCICA, H., PETERSON, W.H. & STEENBOCK, H. *J. Nutr.*, 9: 691.
1935

GOUNELLE DE PONTANEL, H. & DUMAS-ASTIER, M. Les protéines de soja structurées. Accep-
1970 tabilité. *Annls Hyg., langue française, Méd. Nutr.*, 6: 97.

GRÄF, W. VON & DIEHL, M. *Arch. Hyg. Bakt.*, 150: 1.
1966

GREENBLATT, M., MIRVISH, S. & SO BING, T. *J. natn. Cancer Inst.*, 46: 1029.
1971

GREEN, R.G. & EVANS, C.A. *Science, N.Y.*, 92: 154.
1940

GROSBY, D.G. Natural cholinesterase inhibitors in food. *In* National Research Council. Food
1966 Production Committee. *Toxicants occurring naturally in foods.* Washington, D.C.
Publication 1354.

GUBLER, D. *Les protéines texturées.* Paper presented to CPCIA.

GUBLER, T.V.P. As proteinas vegetales estructuradas. *CERDIA*, 13960: 62.
1968

HALIM, A.H., WASSOM, C.E., MITCHELL, H.L. & EDMUNDS, L.K. *J. agric. Fd Chem.*, 21: 1118.
1973

HAMDY, H. *Protéines végétales structurées.* Paper presented to the Salon international de
1968 l'alimentation.

HAMMONDS, T. & CALL, D. *Utilization of protein ingredients in the U.S. food industry.* 2 vols.
1970 Ithaca, New York, State College of Agriculture, Cornell University, Agricultural
Experiment Station.

HASHEM, M. *J. Egypt. med. Ass.*, 41: 149.
1958

HASHIMOTO, Y. & FUSETANI, N. *Nippon Suisan Gakkaishi*, 34: 618.
1968

HASLBECK, M. & MEHNERT, H. *Coll. Int. Chim. café C.r.*, 5: 364. (Published 1973)
1971

HASSAL, C.H., REYLE, K. & FENG, P. *Nature, Lond.*, 173: 356.
1954

HAWKSWORTH, G. & HILL, M.J. *Biochem. J.*, 122: 28.
1971

HEISLER, E.G., CORDING, J. JR. & ACETO, N.C. *J. agric. Fd Chem.*, 21: 970.
1973

HENRY, K. & FORD, J. *J. Sci. Fd Agric.*, 16: 425.
1965

HILKER, D.M. *Int. Z. VitamForsch.*, 38: 387.
1968

HILL, M.J., CROWTHER, J.S., DRASAR, B.S., HAWKSWORTH, G., ARIES, V. & WILLIAMS, R.E.O.
1971 *Lancet*, 95: 1.

HILLER, A. *Ind. aliment. agric..*, 85: 27.
1968

HOCHSTRASSER, K., MUSS, M. & WERLE, E. *Hoppe-Seyler's Z. physiol. Chem.*, 348: 1337.
1967

HOGUE, D.E. *J. Dairy Sci.*, 53: 1135.
1970

HOLLO, J. *Aust. chem. Engng*, 10: 9.
1969

HOPPE, K., KOZLOWSKA, M. & RUTKOWSKI, A. *Milchwissenschaft*, 26: 19.
1971

HORAN, F.E. *Proc. Int. Conf. on Soybean Protein Foods, Peoria, Ill., 1966*, 35: 129. Washington,
1967 D.C., U.S. Agricultural Research Service.

HOVE, E.L., LOHREY, E., URS, M.K. & ALLISON, R.M. *Br. J. Nutr.*, 31: 147.
1974

HOWE, R.W. *Nutr. Abstr. Rev.*, 85: 285.
1965

INSTITUT NATIONAL DE LA RECHERCHE AGRONOMIQUE. *Annls Zootech.*, 20: 5.
1971

INSTITUT NATIONAL DE LA SANTÉ ET DE LA RECHERCHE MÉDICALE. *Colloque sur les effets
1974 physiopathologiques des acides gras à chaîne très longue.* Paris.

ISHIHARA, T., YASUDA, M. & MOROOKA, H. *Nippon Suisan Gakkaishi*, 38: 1281.
1972
ISHIHARA, T., KINARI, H. & YASUDA, M. *Nippon Suisan Gakkaishi*, 39: 55.
1973
ISHIKAWA, S., NAKAMURA, K., SHUDO, K. & KIBASHI, K. *Suisancho Hokkaido-Ku Suisan*
1966 *Kenkynsho Kenkyu Hokaku*, (31): 112.
IWARSSON, K. & NILSSON, P.O. *Acta vet. scand.*, 14: 595.
1973
IWARSSON, K., EKMAN, L., EVERITT, B.R., FIGUEIRAS, H. & NILSSON, P.O. *Acta vet. scand.*, 14:
1973 610.
IWATA, H., OKAMOTO, H. & OHSAWA, Y. *Res. Commun. Chem. Pathol. Pharmacol.*, 5: 673.
1973
JACQUOT, R., TRÉMOLIÈRES, J., GUILLEMET, R. & ERFMANN, R. *Bull. Acad. natn. Méd.*, 128:
1944 608.
JAFFE, W.G. Hemagglutinins. *In* Liener, I.E., ed. *Toxic constituents in plant foodstuffs*, p. 69.
1969 New York, Academic Press.
JAFFE, W.G. Factors affecting the nutritional value of beans. *In* Protein-Calorie Advisory
1973 Group of the United Nations System. *Nutritional improvement of food legumes by
breeding*. New York, United Nations.
JAFFE, W.G. & VEGA, C.L. *J. Nutr.*, 94: 203.
1968
JAFFE, W.G. & BRUCHER, O. *Archos lat.-am. Nutr.*, 22: 267.
1972
JAIN, R.C. *Lancet*, 1: 1240.
1975
JEMMALI, M. *Annls Microbiol.*, 124B: 109.
1973
JESWANI, L.M., LAL, B.M. & PRAKASH, S. *Curr. Sci.*, 39: 518.
1970
JOFFE, A.Z. Toxin production by cereal fungi causing toxic alimentary alenkya in man. *In*
1965 Wogan, G., ed. *Mycotoxins in foodstuffs*, p. 77-85. Cambridge, Mass., MIT Press.
JOHNSON, O.C. *F.D.A. Consumer*, Dec.-Jan.: 4.
1973-74
JOSEPH, A. *Annls Nutr. Aliment.*, 27: 125.
1973
JOURNÉE D'ÉTUDE CONSACRÉE A L'UTILISATION DES OESTROGÈNES EN ÉLEVAGE, 19 mai 1972.
1973 *Exposés*. Alfort, Ecole nationale vétérinaire.
KADKOL, S.B., PINGALE, S.V. & SWAMINATHAN, M. *Bull. cent. Fd. technol. Res. Inst., Mysore,* 6:
1957 30.
KAKADE, M.L. & EVANS, R.J. *J. Nutr.*, 90: 191.
1966
KAKADE, M.L., HOFFA, D.E. & LIENER, I.E. *J. Nutr.*, 103: 1772.
1973
KANOTA, K. *Eisei Shikenjo Hokoku*, 87: 31.
1969
KANOTA, K. Toxic metabolites of *Penicillium roqueforti*. *Proc. Ist. U.S. Jap. Conf. Toxic.*
1970 *Microorganism, 1968*, p. 129.
KAWASAKI, M. & ONO, T. *Bitamin*, 37: 44.
1968
KEELER, R.F. *Clin. Toxicol.*, 5: 529.
1972

KERMODE, G.O. & MCNALLY, H.J. Joint FAO/WHO Food Standards Programme, Codex
1973   Alimentarius Commission. *Nutr. Newsl. (FAO)*, 11 (1): 1-35.

KEYBETS, M.J.H., GROOT, E.H. & KELLER, G.H.M. *Voeding*, 31: 64.
1970

KIES, C. & FOX, H. *J. Fd Sci.*, 36: 941.
1971

KIHLBERG, R. *A. Rev. Microbiol.*, 26: 427.
1972

KINGSBAKER, C.L. *J. Am. Oil Chem. Soc.*, 47: 458/A.
1970

KLOSTERMAN, H.J. *J. agric. Fd Chem.*, 22: 13.
1974

KNEALE, W.A. *Expl Husb.*, (22): 55.
1972

KOBORI, S.O., YOSHIMURA, E. & NAKANE, S. *J. Tokyo Soc. vet. zootech. Sci.*, 20: 1.
1957

KONIJN, A.M., GERSHON, B. & GUGGENHEIM, K. *J. Nutr.*, 103: 378.
1973

KOWALEWSKI, K. *Proc. Soc. exp. Biol. Med.*, 144: 1014.
1973

KRAMER, J.K.G., MAHADEVAN, S., HUNT, J.R., SAUER, F.D., CORNER, A.H. & CHARLTON,
1973   K.M. *J. Nutr.*, 103: 1696.

KRATZER, F.H. & WILLIAMS, D.E. *J. Nutr.*, 36: 297.
1948

KRAYBILL, H.F. & SHIMKIN, A., *Adv. Cancer Res.*, 8: 191.
1964

KREBS, H.A. & MELLANBY, K. *Biochem. J.*, 37: 466.
1943

KREH, K.Q. *Soybean Dig.*, 31(1): 28.
1970

KREHL, W.A., STRONG, M.F. & ELVEHJEM, A.C. *J. biol. Chem.*, 156: 1, 13.
1944

KU, P.K., ELY, W.T., GROCE, A.W. & ULLREY, D.E. *J. Anim. Sci.*, 34: 208.
1972

KU, P.K., MILLER, E.R., WAHLSTROM, R.C., GROCE, A.W., HITCHCOCK, J.P. & ULLREY, D.E.
1973   *J. Anim. Sci.*, 37: 501.

KUNITZ, M. *Science, N.Y.*, 101: 668.
1945

KURISAKI, J., SASAGO, K., TSUGO, T. & YAMAUCHI, K. *Shokukin Eiseigaku Zasshi*, 14: 25.
1973

LACASSAGNE, A. *Vitalstoffe*, 12: 5.
1967

LACHANCE, P.A. *Fd Technol., Champaign*, 24: 239.
1970

LANG, K. *Wld Rev. Nutr. Diet.*, 12: 266.
1970

LAPORTE, J. & TRÉMOLIÈRES, J. *C.r. Séanc. Soc. Biol.*, 156: 1261.
1962

LAQUEUR, G.L., MICKELSEN, O., WHITING, M.G. & KURLAND, L.T. *J. natn. Cancer Inst.*, 31:
1963   919.

LEFEBVRE, J. *Cah. Nutr. Diet.*, 4: 45.
1970
LENNON, I. & TAGLE, M. *Archos lat.-am. Nutr.*, 23: 243.
1973
LEOPOLD, A.C. & ARDREY, R. *Science, N.Y.*, 176: 512.
1972
LEPKOVSKY, S. National Academy of Sciences, Publication 1354, p. 98.
1966
LEPKOVSKY, S., SHAELEFF, W., PETERSON, D. & PERRY, R. *Poultry Sci.*, 29: 208.
1950
LEVINA, E.N., CHEKUNOVA, M.P. & MINKINA, N.A. *Farmak. Toks.*, 36: 620.
1973
L'HIRONDELLE, J., GUILHARD, J., MOREL, C., FREYMUTH, F., SIGNORET, N. & SIGNORET, C.
1971   *Annls Pédiatrie*, 18: 625.
LIENER, I.E. Cyanogenetic glycosides. *In* National Research Council. Food Production Com-
1966   mittee. *Toxicants occurring naturally in foods.* Washington, D.C. Publication 1354.
LIENER, I.E. Antitryptic and other antinutritional factors in legumes. *In* Protein-Calorie Ad-
1973   visory Group of the United Nations System. *Nutritional improvement of food legumes by breeding.* New York, United Nations.
LIENER, I.E. *J. agric. Fd Chem.*, 22: 17.
1974
LIENER, I.E., DEVEL, H.J., JR. & FEVOLD, H.L. *J. Nutr.*, 39: 325.
1949
LIEW, L.S. & CHANG, P. *Asian J. Med.*, 8: 281.
1972
LIJINSKY, W. *Nature, Lond.*, 225: 21.
1970
LIJINSKY, W. *Nature, Lond.*, 239: 165.
1972
LIJINSKY, W. *Science, N.Y.*, 182: 1194.
1973
LINAZASORO, J.M., SANCHEZ MARTIN, J.A. & JIMENEZ-DIAZ, G. *Endocrinology*, 86: 696.
1970
LO, T. & HILL, *J. Sci. Fd Agric.*, 22: 128.
1971
LOEWE, S., LANGE, F. & SPOHR, E. *Biochem. Z.*, 180: 1.
1927
LOHREY, E., TAPPER, B. & HOVE, E.L. *Br. J. Nutr.*, 31: 159.
1974
LONGTON, R.W. *Experientia*, 29: 1013.
1973
LOVENBERG, W. *J. agric. Fd Chem.*, 22: 23.
1974
LU, F.C. *WHO Chronicle*, 28: 8.
1974
LUNA ZENAIDA, G., MARZAN, A.M., MONTILLA, A.A. & CAASI, P. *Philipp. J. Sci.*, 97: 145.
1968
LUND, G. *Fiskeridirektoratets Skrifter,* Serie Teknologiske Undersøkelser, 5.
1972
MAILLARD, L.C. *C.r. hebd Séanc. Acad. Sci., Paris*, 154: 66.
1912

MAINGUY, P. *Recherches historiques sur la concurrence vitale entre les micro-organismes.* Paris.
1949   (Thesis)

MALLET, L., PERDRIAU, L.V. & PERDRIAU, J. *C.r. hebd. Séanc. Acad. Sci., Paris,* 256: 348.
1963

MARQUARDT, P., SCHMIDT, H. & SPATH, M. *Arzneimittel-Forsch.,* 13: 11.
1963

MARTIN, R.E. *Soybean Dig.,* 30: 26.
1970

MASQUELIER, J. The bactericidal action of certain phenolics of grapes and wine. *In* Fairbairn,
1959   J.W. ed. *The pharmacology of plant phenolios,* 123 p. New York and London,
             Academic Press.

MASQUELIER, J. Les antibiotiques naturels des aliments. In *Antibiotiques en agriculture.*
1968   *Comptes rendus du cinquième Symposium du Groupe européen de nutritionnistes.*
             Jouy-en-Josas, 1966, p. 159. Bâle, Karger.

MAURICE, J. & TROCME, S. *C.r. hebd. Séanc. Acad. Agric. Fr.,* 6: 351.
1965

MAURON, J. *Int. Z. VitamForsch.,* 2: 32.
1969

MAYER, K., PAUSE, G. & VETSCH, U. *Obst- u. Gemüse-Verw.-Ind.,* 58: 30.
1973

MCPHILIP, L.J. *R. Soc. Hlth J.,* 90: 237.
1970

MELLANBY, E. *Lancet,* 1: 1290.
1920

MELLANBY, E. *Br. med.* J., 2: 849.
1922

MELLANBY, E. *Br. med. J.,* 4: 895.
1924

MENTZER, C. *Annls Nutr. Aliment.,* 3: 339.
1947

MÉRIMÉE, T.J. & EINEBERG, S.E. *Lancet,* 2: 120.
1973

MEUNIER, P. Les antivitamines. In *Progress in the chemistry of organic natural products,* 9: 88.
1952   Wien, Springer.

MICHAJLOWSKIY, N. & LANGER, P. *Hoppe-Seyler's Z. physiol. Chem.,* 312: 26; 317: 20.
1958-59

MICKELSEN, O. Present knowledge of naturally occurring toxicants in foods. *Nutr. Rev.,* 26:
1968   129.

MICKELSEN, O. & YANG, M.G. *Fedn Proc. Fedn Am. Socs exp. Biol.,* 25: 104.
1966

MIKOLA, J. & SNOLINNA, E.M. *Eur. J. Biochem.,* 9: 555.
1969

MIRVISH, S.S. *J. nat. Cancer Inst.,* 46: 1183.
1971

MOREAU, C. *Moisissures toxiques dans l'alimentation.* Paris, Masson.
1974

MORELON, R. & NIAUSSAT, P. *Cah. Pacif.,* 10: 1.
1967

MORI, K. & MIYASHITA, C. Japanese patent, *Chem. Abstr.,* 80: 36.045.
1974

MORICE, J. L'amélioration génétique du colza. *Journées internationales sur le colza.* Paris,
1970   Institut national de la recherche agronomique. (And personal communication)

MORRIS, M.L., TEETER, S.M. & COLLINS, D.R. *J. Am. vet. med. Ass.*, 158: 477.
1971

MORRISON, J.E. & PIRIE, N.W. *J. Sci. Fd Agric.*, 12: 1.
1961

MOSSE, J. *Note complémentaire sur les concentrés protéiques et les aliments végétaux imitant la*
1970   *viande.* Paris, Institut national de la recherche agronomique.

MUELLER-WECKER, H. & KOFRANYT, E. *Hoppe-Seyler's Z. physiol. Chem.*, 354 (9): 1034.
1973

MURTI, V.V.S. & SESHADRI, T.R. Naturally occurring less common aminoacids of possible
1967   nutritional interest and their simple derivatives. *Nutr. Abstr. Rev.*, 37; 677.

NATIONAL RESEARCH COUNCIL. Food Production Committee. *Toxicants occurring naturally in*
1966   *foods.* Washington, D.C. Publication 1354.

NEEMAN, L., LIFSHITZ, A. & KASHMAN, Y. *Appl. Microbiol.*, 19: 470.
1970

NEVINS, M.P. & GRANT, D.W. *Bull. environ. Contamin. Toxicol.*, 6: 552.
1971

NOYES, R. Protein food supplements. *Fd Process. Rev.*, 3: 302.
1959

NOZDRIN, N.I. *Svinovodstvo*, (9): 31.
1969

Nutr. Rev., 18: 12.
1960

Nutr. Rev., 26: 40.
1968

Nutr. Rev., 30: 221.
1972

Nutr. Rev., 31: 250.
1973a

Nutr. Rev., 31: 308.
1973b

Nutr. Rev., 31: 318.
1973c

Nutr. Rev., 32: 55.
1974

ODELL, A. *Incorporation of protein isolates into meat analogs.* Cambridge, Mass., MIT Press.
1968

OELSHLEGEL, F.J. JR., SCHROEDER, J.R. & STAHMANN, M.A. *J. Sci. Fd Agric.*, 17: 791, 796.
1969

OETTLE, A.G. *S. Afr. med. J.*, 39: 817.
1965

OKE, O.L. *Wld Rev. Nutr. Diet.*, 10: 262.
1969

OLSON, G., PUDELKIEWICZ, W.J. & MATTERSON, C.D. *J. Nutr.*, 30: 199.
1966

OLTERSDORF, U., MILTENBERGER, R. & CREMER, H.D. *Wld Rev. Nutr. Diet.*, 26: 41.
1977

OOMAE, H. *Sekiyu To Sekiyn Kagaku*, 15: 57.
1971

ORGELL, W.H. *Lloydia*, 26: 36.
1963
ORGELL, W.H. & HIBBS, E.T. *Proc. Am. Soc. hort. Sci.*, 83: 651.
1963
OSBORN, T.B. & MENDEL, L.B. *Hoppe-Seyler's Z. physiol. Chemie*, 80: 307.
1912
PARUELLE, J.L., TOULLEC, R., FRANTZEN, J.P. & MATHIEU, C.M. *Annls Zootech.*, 21: 319.
1972
PAYET, M. *Presse méd.*, 73: 1995.
1965
PELLERIN, F. & BOURGAIN, L.P. *Annls pharm. fr.*, 31: 269.
1973
PELTOLA, P. *Acta Endocr.*, 34: 121.
1960
PERRAULT, M. *Sem. thér.*, 41: 284.
1965
PERRAULT, M., BOISSELOT-LEFEBVRE, J. & RATSIMAMANGA, A.R. *Revue Pratn*, 10: 2245.
1960
PERSANOV, V.M. & ANDREEVA, T.F. *Miner. Elem. Mekh. Fotozin.*, 1969: 22-31. (In *Chem.*
1969   *Abstr.*, 74: 121.529, 1971).
PETUELY, F. *Scr. med. Fac. med. Univ. Brun Purkynianae*, 46: 87.
1973
PION, R. & FAUCONNEAU, G. *Amino-acides, Peptides, Protéines*. AEC 6.
1966
PIRIE, N.W. *Science, N.Y.*, 152: 1701.
1966
PIRIE, N.W. *Proc. Nutr. Soc.*, 28: 85.
1969
PIRIE, N.W. *Leaf protein: its agronomy, preparation, quality and use*. Oxford, Blackwell Scien-
1971   tific Publications.
PLANAS, G.M. & KUC', J. *Science*, 162: 1007.
1968
PLUMAS, B. *Cah. Nutr. Diet.*, 6: 49.
1971
POLANOWSKI, A. *Acta biochim. pol.*, 14: 389.
1967
POPE, D.L. *Feedstuffs*, 43: 30.
1971
POULLAIN, B., GUISARD, D. & DEBRY, G. *Nutr. Metab.*, 14: 298.
1972
POZNANSKI, S., BEDNARSKI, W., JAKUBOWSKI, J. & SAWICKI, Z. *Przem. ferment. Rolny*, 17: 27.
1973
PROTEIN-CALORIE ADVISORY GROUP OF THE UNITED NATIONS SYSTEM. *Report on the second*
1971   *meeting of the PAG Ad Hoc Working Group on Single Cell Protein, Moscow,*
         U.S.S.R., 7-10 June 1971. New York, United Nations.
PROTEIN-CALORIE ADVISORY GROUP OF THE UNITED NATIONS SYSTEM. *Nutritional improve-*
1973   *ment of food legumes by breeding. Proceedings of a Symposium sponsored by PAG,*
         Rome, 3-5 July 1972. New York, United Nations.
QUEVAUVILLER, A. *Méd. Afrique noire*, 21: 109.
1974

RACKISS, J.J., HONIG, D.H., SESSA, D.J. & STEGGERDA, F.R. *J. agric. Fd Chem.*, 18: 977.
1970
RAKOSKY, J. *J. agric. Fd Chem.*, 18: 1005.
1970
RAMIREZ, J.S. & MITCHELL, H.L. *J. agric. Fd Chem.*, 8: 593.
1960
RAO, S.L.N., MALATHI, I. & SARMA, P.S. *Wld Rev. Nutr. Diet.*, 10: 214.
1969
RATSIMAMANGA, A.R., MONDAIN-MONVAL-GÉRONDEAU, M. & DIOT, J. *C.r. Séanc. Soc. Biol.*,
1962   156: 1076.
REBSDORF, A. *Nord. Vet Med.*, 25: 168.
1973
REDDY, B.S. & WYNDER, E.L. *J. natn. Cancer Inst.*, 50: 1437.
1973
REDDY, B.S., WEISBURGER, J.H. & WYNDER, E.L. *Science, N.Y.*, 183: 416.
1974
REHR, S.S., JANSEN, D.H. & FEENY, P.P. *Science, N.Y.*, 181: 81.
1973
REINHART, R.R. & SAIR, L. Patent, Quaker Oats Co. and GRIFFITH Laboratories, 1 June 1973.
1971, 1973   *U.S. application 180, No. 134, September 1971.* (In *Chem. Abstr.*, 80: 13.831, 1974)
RÉRAT, A. *Cah. Nutr. Diet.*, 3: 59.
1969
RICHET, C. *C.r. Séanc. Soc. Biol.*, 62: 358.
1907
RIVERS, J.P.W. & HILL, A.W. *Proc. Nutr. Soc.*, 30: 77A.
1971
ROCQUELIN, G., GLUZAN, R., VODOVAR, N. & LEVILLAIN, R. *Cah. Nutr. Diet.*, 8: 103.
1973
ROCQUELIN, G., SERGIEL, J.P., ASTORG, P.O. & CLUZAN, R. *Annls Biol. anim. Biochim. Bio-*
1973   *phys.*, 13: 587.
ROUELLE, H.M. *Méd., Chir., Pharm.*, 40: 59.
1773
RUTKOWSKI, A., KOZLOWSKA, H. & HOPPE, K. *Ernährungsforschung*, 16: 541.
1972
RUTLEDGE, J.E. & LEVI, C.Y. *J. Fd Sci.*, 37: 497.
1972
SAAKADZE, V.P., ALEKSEEVA, O.G. & MANDZHGALADZE, R.N. *Gig. Truda prof. Zabol.*, (1): 10.
1973
SAGHIR, A.R., COWAN, J.W. & SALJI, J.P. *Nature, Lond.*, 87: 211.
1966
SAGHIR, A.R., COWAN, J.W. & SALJI, J.P. *Proc. 3rd Symp. Hum. Nutr. Hlth, Near East, 1967.* (In
1967   *Chem. Abstr.*, 73: 54.116, 1970)
SAINT, W.F. *Soybean Dig.*, 31: 32.
1970
SAKAKI, J. *J. Tokyo med. Soc.*, 5: 1097.
1891
SANDER, J. & SCHWEINSBERG, F. *Chem. Abstr.*, 78: 24.771, 24.772.
1973
SANTARIUS, K. & BELITZ, H.D. *Chem. Mikrobiol. Technol. Lebensmittel*, 2: 56.
1972

SAPEIKA, N. *Food pharmacology.* Springfield, Ill., Thomas.
1969

SAPEIKA, N. *Wld Rev. Nutr. Diet.,* 29: 115.
1978

SAPETTI, C., ARDVINO, E. & DURIO, P. *Folia vet. latina,* 3: 74.
1973

SCHACKLETTE, H.T. *Cadmium in plants.* Washington, D.C., US Geological Survey. Bulletin
1972   1314.

SCHELENZ, R. & DIEHL, J.F. *Z. Lebensmittelunters. u. -Forsch.,* 151: 369.
1973

SCHÜTTE, K. H. & SCHENDEL, H.E. *Nature, Lond.,* 182: 958.
1958

SCLAFAVI, A. *Physiol. Behav.,* 11: 595.
1973

SCOTT, M.L. *J. Nutr.,* 103: 803.
1973

SEDLAK, J., LANGER, P. & MICHAJLOVSKI, J.N. *Bratisl. lék. Listy,* 46: 9.
1966

SEN, N.P., MILES, W.F., DONALDSON, B., PANALAKS, T. & IYENGAR, J.R. *Nature, Lond.,* 245:
1973   104.

SÉNEZ, J.C. Les protéines unicellulaires: place et potentiel des levures cultivées sur alcanes. In
1972   *Les levures cultivées sur alcanes. Symposium d'Aix-en-Provence,* ed by H. Gounelle
         de Pontanel. Paris, Centre de recherches Foch.

SÉNEZ, J.C. *Recl Méd. vét. Ec. Alfort,* 149: 889.
1973

SERGENT, E. *Archs Inst. Pasteur Algér.,* 19: 161.
1941

SERK-HANSSEN, *Archs envir. Hlth,* 20: 729.
1970

SHACKLADY, C.A. & GATUMEL, E. Valeur nutritionnelle des levures cultivées sur alcanes. In
1972   *Les levures cultivées sur alcanes. Symposium d'Aix-en-Provence,* ed by H. Gounelle
         de Pontanel. Paris, Centre de recherches Foch.

SHANK, R.C., BOURGEOIS, C.H., KESCHAMBRAS, N. & CHANDAVIMOL, P. *Fd Cosmet. Toxicol.,*
1971   4: 501.

SHANK, R.C., WOGAN, G.N., GIBSON, J.B. & NONDASUTA, A. *Fd Cosmet. Toxicol.,* 10: 61.
1972

SHARAF, A. *Qualitas Pl. Mater. veg.,* 14: 267.
1967

SHARAF, A. & GOMARA, N. *Qualitas Pl. Mater. veg.,* 20: 279.
1971

SHARAF, A., ABDOU, I., HASSAN, M., YOSSIF, M. & NEGM, S.A. *Qualitas P. Mater. veg.,* 17: 313.
1969

SHIRAISHI, Y., SHIROTORI, T. & TAKABATAKE, E. *Shokukin eiseigaki zasshi.,* 14: 173.
1973

SIMS, R.P.A. *J. Am. Oil Chem. Soc.,* 48: 733.
1971

SINGH, N. *Report.* Mysore, Central Food Technological Research Institute.
1969

SINGH, P.P. *Qualitas Pl. Mater. veg.,* 22: 335.
1973

SINGH, P.P., KOTHARI, L.K. & SHARMA, H.S. *Asian med. J.*, 16: 287.
1973
SINGSEN, E.P., POTTER, L.M., BUNNELL, R.H., MATTERSON, L.D., STINSON, L., AMATO, S.V. &
1955   JUNGHERR, E.L. *Poultry Sci.*, 34: 1234.
SLAVENAS, J. *Chem. Abstr.*, 66: 35.398.
1967
SMITH, T.A. *Phytochemistry*, 12: 2093.
1973
SNIGORSKA, B. & BARTEL, H. *Folia morph.*, 29: 353.
1970
SOMOGYI, J.C. *J. Vitam.*, 17: 165.
1971
SOMOGYI, J.C. Antivitamins. In *Toxicants occurring naturally in foods*, p. 254. Washington,
1973   D.C., National Academy of Sciences.
SOMOGYI, J.C. *Wld Rev. Nutr. Diet.*, 29: 42.
1978
SPETOLLI, P. *Industrie agr.*, 9: 1.
1971a
SPETOLLI, P. *Industrie agr.*, 9: 42.
1971b
STAHMANN, M.A., HUEBNER, C.F. & LINK, K.P. *J. biol. Chem.*, 138: 513.
1941
STANDARA, S. & CHURY, J. *Acta vet., Brno*, 41: 251.
1973
STARE, F.J. *Eating for good health*. Rev. ed. New York, Cornerstone Library.
1969
STERNBERG, M., KIM, C.Y. & SCHWENDE, F.J. *Science*, 190: 992.
1975
STEVENS, R.H. & HARMON, B.G. Ger. Offen 2.163.364 (Cl. A 23 K), 13 July 1972. *U.S.*
1970, 1972   *application 100587, 22 December 1970.*
STOESSL, A., UNWIN, C.H. & WARD, E.W.B. *Phytopathology*, 63: 1225.
1973
STOEWSAND, G.S. *N.Y. State Ass. Milk Food Sanit. A. Rep., 1972*, 46: 27.
1972
Symposium on natural food toxicants. *J. agric. Fd Chem.*, 17: 413.
1969
TADA, M., SENO, F., MURATA, T. & KAWASAKI, A. *Nippon Kakin Gakkaishi*, 9: 17.
1972
TADA, M., FURNICHI, H., SENO, F., BANSHO, H., YAMANAKA, K., IWASE, N. & YAHATA, S.
1973   *Nippon Kakin Gakkaishi*, 10: 93.
TANNER, J.T. *Science, N.Y.*, 177: 1102.
1972
TAO, M., BOULET, M., BRISSON, G.J., HUANG, K.H., RIEL, R.R. & JULIEN, J.P. *J. Can. Inst. Fd*
1972   *Sci. Technol.*, 5: 50.
TARANOV, M.T. & VLADIMIROV, V.L. *Dokl. vses. Akad. sel'.-khoz. Nauk*, (10): 22.
1971
TATSUNO, T. *Fd Cosmet. Toxicol.*, 2: 678.
1964
TAUBER, H., KLEINER, I.S. & MISKIND, D. *J. biol. Chem.*, 110: 211.
1935

TÄUFEL, K. *Die Nahrung*, 14: 229.
1970

TERAUCHI, Y., WADA, C. & OHYAMA, T. *J. Jap. Soc. int. Med.*, 16: 825.
1928

TERROINE, E.F. *Le métabolisme nucléique*. Paris, Centre national de la recherche scientifique.
1960

THAYER, P.S. & KENSLER, C.J. *Toxic. appl. Pharmac.*, 25: 169.
1973

THOMAS, B., ROUGHAN, J.A., & WATTERS, E. *J. Sci. Fd Agric.*, 24: 447.
1973

THOMPSON, J.F., CLAYTON, J.M. & SMITH, I.K. New naturally occurring amino-acids. *A. Rev.*
1969   *Biochem.*, 38: 137.

THULIN, W.W. & KURAMOTO, S. *Fd Technol.*, 21: 64.
1967

TILGNER, D. J. *Chem. Abstr.*, 75: 18.981.
1971

TJOSTEM, J.L. *Proc. Iowa Acad. Sci.*, 72: 51. (Published 1967)
1965

TTUHAUT, R. *Annls Falsif. Fraudes*, 48: 1.
1955

TRUHAUT, R. *Bull. Inst. natn. Santé Rech. méd.*, 21: 1063.
1966

TURRO, E.J. *U.S. Patent 3,320,070.*
1969

TYLER, G. *Ambio*, 1: 52.
1972

UNESCO. *Symposium sur les aflatoxines, Paris, septembre 1976*. Paris.
1976

US DEPARTMENT OF AGRICULTURE. ECONOMIC RESEARCH SERVICE. Marketing Research Re-
1972   port 947.

VAGUE, R. & GARRIGUES, R. *Annls Endocr.*, 18: 745.
1957

VALFRÈ, F., BOSI, G. & BELLEZA, P. *Selez. suinavicunicola*, (11): 1-15.
1977

VAN DER VELDEN, M., KINTHAERT, J., ORTS, S. & ERMANS, A.M. *Br. J. Nutr.*, 30: 511.
1973

VAN DER WAL, P., VAN HELLEMOND, K.K., SHACKLADY, C.A. & VAN DER WEERDEN, E.J. *Yeast*
1971   *grown on gas oil in animal nutrition. 2. In rations for pigs.* Document, 10th Interna-
          tional Congress of Animal Husbandry, Paris-Versailles, 1971.

VAN STRATUM, P., RUDRUM, M., TENHOOR, F., WILSON, R. & PIKAAR, N.A. *Proc. Nutr. Soc.*,
1978   37: 11A.

VAN VEEN, A.G. Toxic properties of some unusual foods. *In* National Research Council. Food
1966   Production Committee. *Toxicants occurring naturally in foods.* Washington, D.C.
          Publication 1354.

VELU, H. *C.r. Séanc. Soc. Biol.*, 108: 377, 750.
1931

VLITOS, A.J. *Rev. Nutr. Res.*, 21: 13.
1960

VOGT, K. & DE KARG, H. *Z. Tierphysiol. Tierernähr. Futtermittelk.*, 28: 1.
1971

VON PUFENDORF, U. *Cérès*, 7: 49.
1974
WALKER, D., HORAN, F. & BURKET, R. *Fd Technol., Champaign*, 25: 55.
1971
WANG, L.C. *Pl. Physiol.*, 50: 152.
1972
WARREN, H.V., DELAVAULT, R.E. & FLETCHER, K.W. *Can. Min. metall. Bull.*, July 1971: 1.
1971
WASLIEN, C.I., CALLOWAY, D.H., MORGEN, S. & COSTA, F. *J. Fd Sci.*, 35: 294.
1970
WATERLOW, J.C. *Br. J. Nutr.*, 16: 531.
1962
WEINSTEIN, D., MAUER, I. & SOLOMON HERVEY, M. *Mutat. Res.*, 16: 391.
1972
WEISBURGER, J.H. *Cancer*, 28: 60.
1971
WEISS, M. *Oléagineux*, 23: 201.
1968
WENGER INTERNATIONAL INC., KANSAS CITY, MISSOURI. *In* Factors conditioning the produc-
1975   tion of conventional and non-conventional proteins. *Folia vet.*, 6 (Suppl. 1): 65.
WESTEEN, R.S. & KURAMOTO, S. *U.S. Patent 3,118,959.*
1964
WILDING, M.D. *J. Am. Oil Chem. Soc.*, 47: 398.
1970
WILLS, J.H. JR. Seafood toxins. *In* National Research Council. Food Production Committee.
1966   *Toxicants occurring naturally in foods.* Washington, D.C. Publication 1354.
WINKLER, W.O. *J. Ass. off. agric. Chem.*, 41: 282.
1958
WOGAN, G., ed. *Mycotoxins in foodstuffs.* Cambridge, Mass., MIT Press.
1965
WOLF, W.J. *J. agric. Fd Chem.*, 18: 969.
1970
WOLF, W.J. & COWAN, J.C. *Fd Technol., Champaign*, 25.
1971
WOLFF, I.A. & WASSERMAN, A.E. *Science, N.Y.*, 177: 15.
1972
WOLFF, J. & VARRONE, S. *Endocrinology*, 85: 410.
1969
WOODARD, J.C. & SHORT, D.D. *J. Nutr.*, 103: 569.
1973
WOODROOF, J.G. *Peanuts: production, processing, products.* Westport, Conn., Avi.
1966
WOLLEY, D.W. *J. biol. Chem.*, 141: 997.
1941
WOOLLEY, D.W. & LANGSWORTH, L.G. *J. biol. Chem.*, 142: 285, 290.
1942
WORLD HEALTH ORGANIZATION. *The public health aspects of the use of antibiotics in food and
1962   feedstuffs.* Geneva. Technical Report Series No. 260.
WORLD HEALTH ORGANIZATION. *Principles for pre-clinical testing of drug safety.* Geneva.
1966   Technical Report Series No. 341.

WORLD HEALTH ORGANIZATION. *WHO Chronicle*, 27: 580.
1973
WORLD HEALTH ORGANIZATION. Pharmacogenetics — the influence of heredity on the re-
1974   sponse to drugs. *WHO Chronicle*, 28: 25.
WOROWSKI, K. & FABISZEWSKI, R. *Acta physiol. pol.*, 24: 361.
1973
WRIGHT, E. *Nature, Lond.*, 181: 1602.
1958
YAKOVENKO, V.A., LITVINOV, A.M. & STOYANOVA, A.A. *Izv. vyssh. ucheb. Zaved. Pishch.*
1973   *Teckhnol.*, 1973 (4): 17.
YAROV, I.I., BASARGIN, N.N. & SHCHRBAK, L.I. *Vestn. sel'.-khoz. Nauki, Mosk.*, (2): 50.
1973
YASUI, T. & IWAMATSU, K. *Chem. Abstr.*, 78: 122.937.
1972
YOSHIDA, M. *Sekiyn To Sekiyn Kagaku*, 16: 137.
1972
YOSHIDA, M., TADA, M., BANSHO, H., MATSUSHIMA, M., OGATA, K., IINO, M. & UMEDA, I.
1972   *Japan. Poultry Sci.*, 9: 173.
YOSHIDA, M., TADA, M., BANSHO, H., MATSUSHIMA, M., KOBA, K., IINO, M. & UMEDA, I. *Japan.*
1973   *Poultry Sci.*, 10: 63.
ZAREL, J., KHYAMBASHI, H., ENAMI, A., FARIVAR, H., MONTAMEDI, G., HEDAYAT, H., HEK-
1972   MATAYAR, F. & BAŘNETT, R. *Acta biochim. Iran*, 9: 74.
ZIEMBA, J.V. *Food Engng*, 41: 72.
1969
ZUBER, R., BOVAY, E., TSCHANNEN, W. & QUINCHE, J.P. *Rech. agron. suisse*, 9 (fasc. 1): 83.
1970

FAO SALES AGENTS AND BOOKSELLERS

Algeria	Société nationale d'édition et de diffusion, 92, rue Didouche Mourad, Algiers.
Argentina	Editorial Hemisferio Sur S.A., Librería Agropecuaria, Pasteur 743, 1028 Buenos Aires.
Australia	Hunter Publications, 58A Gipps Street, Collingwood, Vic. 3066; Australian Government Publishing Service, P.O. Box 84, Canberra, A.C.T. 2600; and Australian Government Service Bookshops at 12 Pirie Street, Adelaide, S.A.; 70 Alinga Street, Canberra, A.C.T.; 162 Macquarie Street, Hobart, Tas.; 347 Swanson Street, Melbourne, Vic.; 200 St. Georges Terrace, Perth, W.A.; 309 Pitt Street, Sydney, N.S.W.; 294 Adelaide Street, Brisbane, Qld.
Austria	Gerold & Co., Buchhandlung und Verlag, Graben 31, 1011 Vienna.
Bangladesh	ADAB, 79 Road 11A, P.O. Box 5045, Dhanmondi, Dacca.
Belgium	Service des publications de la FAO, M.J. de Lannoy, 202, avenue du Roi, 1060 Brussels. CCP 000-0808993-13.
Bolivia	Los Amigos del Libro. Perú 3712, Casilla 450, Cochabamba; Mercado 1315, La Paz; René Moreno 26, Santa Cruz; Junín esq. 6 de Octubre, Oruro.
Brazil	Livraria Mestre Jou, Rua Guaipá 518, São Paulo 05089; Rua Senador Dantas 19-S205/206, 20.031 Rio de Janeiro; PRODIL, Promoção e Dist. de Livros Ltda., Av. Venáncio Aires 196, Caixa Postal 4005, 90.000 Porto Alegre; A NOSSA LIVRARIA, CLS 104, Bloco C, Lojas 18/19, 70.000 Brasilia, D.F.
Brunei	SST Trading Sdn. Bhd., Bangunan Tekno No. 385, Jln 5/59, P.O. Box 227, Petaling Jaya, Selangor.
Canada	Renouf Publishing Co. Ltd, 2182 St Catherine West, Montreal, Que. H3H 1M7.
Chile	Tecnolibro S.A., Merced 753, entrepiso 15, Santiago.
China	China National Publications Import Corporation, P.O. Box 88, Beijing.
Colombia	Editorial Blume de Colombia Ltda., Calle 65 N° 16-65, Apartado Aéreo 51340, Bogotá D.E.
Costa Rica	Librería, Imprenta y Litografía Lehmann S.A., Apartado 10011, San José.
Cuba	Empresa de Comercio Exterior de Publicaciones, O'Reilly 407 Bajos entre Aguacate y Compostela, Havana.
Cyprus	MAM, P.O. Box 1722, Nicosia.
Czechoslovakia	ARTIA, Ve Smeckach 30, P.O. Box 790, 111 27 Prague 1.
Denmark	Munksgaard Export and Subscription Service, 35 Nørre Søgade, DK 1370 Copenhagen K.
Dominican Rep.	Fundación Dominicana de Desarrollo, Casa de las Gárgolas, Mercedes 4, Apartado 857, Zona Postal 1, Santo Domingo.
Ecuador	Su Librería Cía. Ltda., García Moreno 1172 y Mejía, Apartado 2556, Quito; Chimborazo 416, Apartado 3565, Guayaquil.
El Salvador	Librería Cultural Salvadoreña S.A. de C.V., Calle Arce 423, Apartado Postal 2296, San Salvador.
Finland	Akateeminen Kirjakauppa, 1 Keskuskatu, P.O. Box 128, 00101 Helsinki 10.
France	Editions A. Pedone, 13, rue Soufflot, 75005 Paris.
Germany, F.R.	Alexander Horn Internationale Buchhandlung, Spiegelgasse 9, Postfach 3340, 6200 Wiesbaden.
Ghana	Fides Enterprises, P.O. Box 14129, Accra; Ghana Publishing Corporation, P.O. Box 3632, Accra.
Greece	G.C. Eleftheroudakis S.A., International Bookstore, 4 Nikis Street, Athens (T-126); John Mihalopoulos & Son S.A., International Booksellers, 75 Hermou Street, P.O. Box 73, Thessaloniki.
Guatemala	Distribuciones Culturales y Técnicas "Artemis", 5a. Avenida 12-11, Zona 1, Apartado Postal 2923, Guatemala.
Guinea-Bissau	Conselho Nacional da Cultura, Avenida da Unidade Africana, C.P. 294, Bissau.
Guyana	Guyana National Trading Corporation Ltd, 45-47 Water Street, P.O. Box 308, Georgetown.
Haiti	Librairie "A la Caravelle", 26, rue Bonne Foi, B.P. 111, Port-au-Prince.
Hong Kong	Swindon Book Co., 13-15 Lock Road, Kowloon.
Hungary	Kultura, P.O. Box 149, 1389 Budapest 62.
Iceland	Snaebjörn Jónsson and Co. h.f., Hafnarstraeti 9, P.O. Box 1131, 101 Reykjavik.
India	Oxford Book and Stationery Co., Scindia House, New Delhi 110001; 17 Park Street, Calcutta 700016.
Indonesia	P.T. Sari Agung, 94 Kebon Sirih, P.O. Box 411, Djakarta.
Iraq	National House for Publishing, Distributing and Advertising, Jamhuria Street, Baghdad.
Ireland	The Controller, Stationery Office, Dublin 4.
Italy	Distribution and Sales Section, Food and Agriculture Organization of the United Nations, Via delle Terme di Caracalla, 00100 Rome; Libreria Scientifica Dott. Lucio de Biasio "Aeiou", Via Meravigli 16, 20123 Milan; Libreria Commissionaria Sansoni S.p.A. "Licosa", Via Lamarmora 45, C.P. 552, 50121 Florence.
Japan	Maruzen Company Ltd, P.O. Box 5050, Tokyo International 100-31.
Kenya	Text Book Centre Ltd, Kijabe Street, P.O. Box 47540, Nairobi.
Kuwait	Saeed & Samir Bookstore Co. Ltd. P.O. Box 5445, Kuwait.
Luxembourg	Service des publications de la FAO, M.J. de Lannoy, 202, avenue du Roi, 1060 Brussels (Belgium).

FAO SALES AGENTS AND BOOKSELLERS

Malaysia
SST Trading Sdn. Bhd., Bangunan Tekno No. 385, Jln 5/59, P.O. Box 227, Petaling Jaya, Selangor.

Mauritius
Nalanda Company Limited, 30 Bourbon-Street, Port Louis.

Mexico
Dilitsa S.A., Puebla 182-D, Apartado 24-448, Mexico 7, D.F.

Morocco
Librairie "Aux Belles Images", 281, avenue Mohammed V, Rabat.

Netherlands
Keesing Boeken V.B., Joan Muyskenweg 22, 1096 CJ Amsterdam.

New Zealand
Government Printing Office. Government Printing Office Bookshops: Retail Bookshop, 25 Rutland Street, Mail Orders, 85 Beach Road, Private Bag C.P.O., Auckland; Retail, Ward Street, Mail Orders, P.O. Box 857, Hamilton; Retail, Mulgrave Street (Head Office), Cubacade World Trade Centre, Mail Orders, Private Bag, Wellington; Retail, 159 Hereford Street, Mail Orders, Private Bag, Christchurch; Retail, Princes Street, Mail Orders, P.O. Box 1104, Dunedin.

Nigeria
University Bookshop (Nigeria) Limited, University of Ibadan, Ibadan.

Norway
Johan Grundt Tanum Bokhandel, Karl Johansgate 41-43, P.O. Box 1177 Sentrum, Oslo 1.

Pakistan
Mirza Book Agency, 65 Shahrah-e-Quaid-e-Azam, P.O. Box 729, Lahore 3.

Panama
Distribuidora Lewis S.A., Edificio Dorasol, Calle 25 y Avenida Balboa, Apartado 1634, Panama 1.

Paraguay
Agencia de Librerías Nizza S.A., Tacuarí 144, Asunción.

Peru
Librería Distribuidora "Santa Rosa", Jirón Apurímac 375, Casilla 4937, Lima 1.

Philippines
The Modern Book Company Inc., 922 Rizal Avenue, P.O. Box 632, Manila.

Poland
Ars Polona, Krakowskie Przedmiescie 7, 00-068 Warsaw.

Portugal
Livraria Bertrand, S.A.R.L., Rua João de Deus, Venda Nova, Apartado 37, 2701 Amadora Codex; Livraria Portugal, Dias y Andrade Ltda., Rua do Carmo 70-74, Apartado 2681, 1117 Lisbon Codex; Edições ITAU, Avda. da República 46/A-r/c Esqdo., Lisbon 1.

Korea, Rep. of
Eul-Yoo Publishing Co. Ltd, 46-1 Susong-Dong, Jongro-Gu, P.O. Box Kwang-Wha-Moon 362, Seoul.

Romania
Ilexim, Calea Grivitei N° 64-66, B.P. 2001, Bucharest.

Saudi Arabia
The Modern Commercial University, P.O. Box 394, Riyadh.

Sierra Leone
Provincial Enterprises, 26 Garrison Street, P.O. Box 1228, Freetown.

Singapore
MPH Distributors (S) Pte. Ltd, 71/77 Stamford Road, Singapore 6; Select Books Pte. Ltd, 215 Tanglin Shopping Centre, 19 Tanglin Road, Singapore 1024; SST Trading Sdn. Bhd., Bangunan Tekno No. 385, Jln 5/59, P.O. Box 227, Petaling Jaya, Selangor.

Somalia
"Samater's", P.O. Box 936, Mogadishu.

Spain
Mundi Prensa Libros S.A., Castelló 37, Madrid 1; Librería Agrícola, Fernando VI 2, Madrid 4.

Sri Lanka
M.D. Gunasena & Co. Ltd, 217 Olcott Mawatha, P.O. Box 246, Colombo 11.

Sudan
University Bookshop, University of Khartoum, P.O. Box 321, Khartoum.

Suriname
VACO n.v. in Suriname, Dominee Straat 26, P.O. Box 1841, Paramaribo.

Sweden
C.E. Fritzes Kungl. Hovbokhandel, Regeringsgatan 12, P.O. Box 16356, 103 27 Stockholm.

Switzerland
Librairie Payot S.A., Lausanne et Genève; Buchhandlung und Antiquariat Heinimann & Co., Kirchgasse 17, 8001 Zurich.

Thailand
Suksapan Panit, Mansion 9, Rajadamnern Avenue, Bangkok.

Togo
Librairie du Bon Pasteur, B.P. 1164, Lomé.

Tunisia
Société tunisienne de diffusion, 5, avenue de Carthage, Tunis.

United Kingdom
Her Majesty's Stationery Office, 49 High Holborn, London WC1V 6HB (callers only); P.O. Box 569, London SE1 9NH (trade and London area mail orders); 13a Castle Street, Edinburgh EH2 3AR; 41 The Hayes, Cardiff CF1 1JW; 80 Chichester Street, Belfast BT1 4JY; Brazennose Street, Manchester M60 8AS; 258 Broad Street, Birmingham B1 2HE; Southey House, Wine Street, Bristol BS1 2BQ.

Tanzania, United Rep. of
Dar es-Salaam Bookshop, P.O. Box 9030, Dar es-Salaam; Bookshop, University of Dar es-Salaam, P.O. Box 893, Morogoro.

United States of America
UNIPUB, 345 Park Avenue South, New York, N.Y. 10010.

Uruguay
Librería Agropecuaria S.R.L., Alzaibar 1328, Casilla de Correos 1755, Montevideo.

Venezuela
Blume Distribuidora S.A., Gran Avenida de Sabana Grande, Residencias Caroni, Local 5, Apartado 50.339, 1050-A Caracas.

Yugoslavia
Jugoslovenska Knjiga, Trg. Republike 5/8, P.O. Box 36, 11001 Belgrade; Cankarjeva Zalozba, P.O. Box 201-IV, 61001 Ljubljana; Prosveta, Terazije 16, P.O. Box 555, 11001 Belgrade.

Zambia
Kingstons (Zambia) Ltd, Kingstons Building, President Avenue, P.O. Box 139, Ndola.

Other countries
Requests from countries where sales agents have not yet been appointed may be sent to: Distribution and Sales Section, Food and Agriculture Organization of the United Nations, Via delle Terme di Caracalla, 00100 Rome, Italy.

SOCIAL SCIENCE LIBRARY

Oxford University Library Services
Manor Road
Oxford OX1 3UQ
Tel: (2)71093 (enquiries and renewals)
http://www.ssl.ox.ac.uk

This is a NORMAL LOAN item.

We will email you a reminder before this item is due.

Please see http://www.ssl.ox.ac.uk/lending.html
for details on:

- loan policies; these are also displayed on the notice boards and in our library guide.

- how to check when your books are due back.

- how to renew your books, including information on the maximum number of renewals. Items may be renewed if not reserved by another reader. Items must be renewed before the library closes on the due date.

- level of fines; fines are charged on overdue books.

Please note that this item may be recalled during Term.

Foto-Tipo-lito SAGRAF - Napoli